Introducing the
Apple® Macintosh™

Howard W. Sams & Co., Inc.

4300 WEST 62ND ST. INDIANAPOLIS, INDIANA 46268 USA

Edward S. Connolly is a well known technical writer and engineer, and recognized expert on the fields of system integration and operation. He has more than ten years experience in the computer industry which included a stint as technical features editor for *Electronic Design*, a Hayden publication. He is an avid amateur radio operator (N2CDS), and when not writing about systems, or designing specialized test equipment, he restores Corvairs. Mr. Connolly frequently consults to various companies on system integration problems and special test instrumentation requirements.

Philip Lieberman is the founder of the consulting firm of Lieberman & Associates in Los Angeles, California. His firm specializes in technical writing and designing state-of-the-art products. Mr. Lieberman has extensive experience in the design and implementation of microprocessors ranging from 4-bit to 32-bit. He has developed real-time multitasking operating systems and application software for a wide range of products.

Mr. Lieberman's application experience includes the development of products ranging from electronic test equipment to interactive graphics and CAD systems. His responsibilities have included product development from concepts and design to manufacturing and field tests. His hobbies include sailing and amateur radio.

Introducing the Apple® Macintosh™

by

Edward S. Connolly

and

Philip Lieberman

Photography by *John Brenners Photography,*
Berkeley, CA.
Dowsing Photography Studios
Torrance, CA.

FIRST EDITION
FIRST PRINTING—1984

International Standard Book Number: 0-672-22361-9
Library of Congress Catalog Card Number: 84-50035

Edited by *Francisco Pflaum*

Printed in the United States of America.

Contents

Acknowledgments

We wish to thank Guy Kawasaki, Caroline Rose, and the countless others at Apple who merit special commendation for providing the literature, interviews, and countless hours of help.

Thank you, Katie Cadigan at Regis-McKenna for your help with the photography. Francisco Pflaum (who burned midnight oil editing) has our appreciation for his keen eye. Nancy Ong, who provided constant support and encouragement throughout the project. Doris Lieberman, who provided invaluable assistance and encouragement.

Finally, our greatest acknowledgment to all the people at Apple who gave life to Mac—it really is a fabulous machine.

Ed Connolly
Phil Lieberman

The MacForeword

A Look at What's on the Apple Tree

This book is a non-computer book written about the most exciting computer yet created: the Apple Macintosh. Although this book gives you a detailed description of the newest Apple creation, it was created, like the Macintosh, for those of you who are wary of pocket calculators, digital watches, and things that whir, buzz, and otherwise clutter your life with technology. You will thus appreciate the tact taken to ease you into the system and how well the Macintosh fits into your normal life style.

However, if you're technically experienced, this book holds fascination for you also.

But don't be mistaken. *Introducing the Apple Macintosh* isn't a programmer's reference, a hardware bits and bytes description, nor is it a detailed user's guide. Rather, this book, like the computer, is a tool that will help your transition from a slow-paced desktop-bound, muddled worker, to a fully productive knowledge worker ready to compete in the eighties. In addition, this book shows you how technology, when properly applied, removes the uncertainty of change.

The elements that you will find in this book include:

- The design philosophy behind Macintosh
- The physical structure of the computer
- An understanding of MacSoftware
- A look at accessories

In addition, this book reveals, with the generous help of Macintosh, how the computer behaves in relationship to people. And why you are an ideal candidate to own one.

As you progress window by information window through this MacBook, you will find out how a wooden, or for that matter a metal desktop, can be transformed into a productivity machine that matches your ability to think, assimilate, and initiate information and ideas.

You will learn new ideas and words such as paradigm, icon, window, and mouse. You will also discover how to point—not with your finger, but with your mind.

As you proceed, new vistas will open up for you.

Yes, you can learn to draw; or, if you have the urge, play a game, paint your idea for tomorrow's presentation; or put together a scrapbook of ideas, important notes, poems, or things to do.

This book, like Macintosh, has been created for you. It is meant to be read for fun, to be studied, and to be savored. It was meant to stimulate thinking, to excite, and remove fears of the unknown.

Though we had the advantage of a machine, and the resources of Apple to assist us, the learning of Macintosh was a discovery process. Not because the machine is complicated—quite the contrary. Rather, it was discovering that technology doesn't need to be complicated.

We also found that we were met with a new challenge: describing that which is self-evident without confusion. We hope that you will find our efforts a success.

Edward S. Connolly
Philip Lieberman

The MacIntroduction

The Blossoming of an Apple

Macintosh blossomed three years ago at Apple as an engineer's personal project. True to the normal tempo of the operation of the forward thinking computer company, it gained adherents. As more core people learned of the project, the excitement grew greater. Quickly, the very core group—and especially Apple Chairman Steve Jobs—recognized that it was an idea that would soon start a new direction for the company. Thus the stage was set for the creation of what was soon to become the most significant and dynamic personal system ever conceived.

Not unlike any creative endeavor, the creation of Macintosh required the combination of brilliant young talent with a freedom of thinking. This, in turn, was to form the basis and operating concept of Macintosh.

The creative drama took place in pristine engineering labs, on breathtaking California hillsides, secluded beach retreats, and within overseas conference rooms.

Macintosh wasn't an old man's dream. Rather, the idea, and the actual machine, speaks of youth—the present and the future. All of the designers—like the two wizards—Steve Jobs and Steve Wozniak, who created the first Apple computer—are under 30 years of age. Some are still too close to adolescence to forget it.

Altruism, imagination, and whimsy characterize not only the approach to the project, but the entire corporate environment. To an extent, so does arrogance. Only true believers work for Apple and they are idealists and ascetics, but they worry about the paint on their BMWs.

The people in the Apple Orchard, the makers of Macintosh's, Lisas and other yet unnamed exciting computers, are the new young turks of the information age and each of the young turks brought an idea and new concept to the development of Macintosh.

As with the development of any high-technology product, decisions were needed as to where it fit in the market, and who would use it. The design team knew because they themselves represented the new breed of computer user: the knowledge worker.

Taking this into account, the design team had several tasks before it. These included defining exactly what a knowledge worker was, and determining what that worker needed, now and in the future, to reach the climax of productivity.

By establishing the right ground rules and making the determinations of whom the machine would be for, and what it should achieve, the design process reached a fever pitch.

More than $50 million has been invested in Macintosh. Of this $20 million was for a new fully automated production facility modeled on Japanese factories. This plant, when run at full tilt, can build a Macintosh in 27 seconds. And operating three shifts a day means that the bushels will be full.

Moreover, Apple borrowed from the basic design of their computers and made this newest Apple Orchard modular. Thus, it can be cloned quickly to meet production demands.

Keeping with the high energy tempo of the company, the senior management team decided that no expense would be spared in the design of the system, production facilities, or any support elements for the machine.

Considerable resources were applied to bring the footprint of the computer, the area it occupies on a desktop, down to the size of a standard sheet of paper. Curiously, in focus group reviews of the machine, this marvelous feat of condensation and integration worked against the unit. When presented with a much bulkier personal computer and the diminutive Macintosh, people without computer experience surveyed in the focus groups tended to believe that the larger machine could do more because of its size. They were way off base.

Part of the MacMagic was achieved by adding over 480 new instructions to augment the 56 basic instructions of the system 68000 microprocessor which are resident within 64,000 bytes (characters) of Read Only Memory (ROM) within Macintosh. These are calls to the so-called User Interface Toolbox and the QuickDraw graphics package that eliminate mind-boggling program chores and staggering memory demands on application software. The entire core of this intricate system is written entirely in the native tongue of the computer's internal microprocessor engine.

No chances were taken in the critical process of developing the internal engine software. When necessary, the MacEngineers painstakingly optimized each tiny verb and nuance of the magic code that makes the machine go. To borrow from an earlier era of technological triumph, they worked until everything was A-OK.

Interestingly, the real magic behind Mac is software, even though the hardware (the physical nuts and bolts) is critical. But critical only from the standpoint of making the software optimum, as far as the user is concerned.

Even though this philosophy of optimization is carried to the nth degree, up to and including ensuring that proper software links exist between the hardware and user software, no applications come bundled with the Macintosh.

By maintaining an open software environment, you, the MacUser, aren't burdened with software that might not be needed. Moreover, it encourages independent software development, rather than competing against it. The view at Apple is this: Macintosh is the new industry standard. First there was the Apple II, then the IBM PC. Now Macintosh eclipses them both in performance. And it matches its performance with equally impressive pricing.

To stimulate gray matter (often called MacThinking) outside Cupertino, two dozen universities around the country were selected to receive large numbers of machines at very reduced cost in return for a pledge that pioneer application programs will run on the Macintosh—no strings attached. As a result, some extraordinary vertical programs are rapidly becoming available from fertile environments that cannot be duplicated in the commercial sector.

An ambitious project at the University of Rochester, for example, applies the Macintosh stipend for music investigation. At Harvard and Yale, law programs are being created. And Reed College sponsors physics program research. The dream continues even as the machine passes from the Apple designer to the knowledge worker.

Further, commercial software houses seem to confirm Macintosh as the emerging standard program environment. More than 100 independent suppliers are at work on programs for the Macintosh. In addition, this establishes credentials for the 3½-inch disk drive employed by the Macintosh, in lieu of conventional 5¼-inch floppy-disk drives.

To gain international acceptance of Macintosh, Apple is building new intermediary software firms that translate domestic programs for overseas markets. In addition, wherever possible, English messages have been replaced by icons that conform to international conventions for graphic symbols. And even with all that, more blossoms are blooming on the Apple tree.

Even though the spotlight is on Mac in this book, it only represents a small link in a growing matrix of ideas and information processing concepts. The Apple 32-bit family also incorporates several improved versions of the Lisa computer with integral hard-disk drives as well as 3½-inch disk drives that accept Macintosh software. The Lisas are the development bed for Macintosh programs. Tying the family together to share resources is a two-wire physical interconnection scheme. This "network" supports up to 32 user locations called *nodes*—other computers are to be supported on a speedy (230.4 Kbits/sec) information link that can be up to 1000 feet from end to end.

This not only means that you, the knowledge worker, can be linked to other knowledge workers, but also share resources. These resources include such items as a laser printer, high-capacity disk drives capable of storing millions of pieces of information, specialized communication devices, and the list goes on, even to devices not yet conceived of. To meet the needs of the emerging electronic office, the 32-bit family scheme combines with the latest techniques of *Private Automatic Branch Exchange (PABX)* telephone systems. This will eventually open up a communications gateway to other information environments.

To match the needs of emerging and existing technologies, the 32-bit scheme offers compatibility with such network methods as: Ethernet, SNA, and other specialized communication protocols, in addition to the forthcoming IBM local-area-network standard that is yet to be defined.

So Macintosh, as part of an overall plan for the office, represents a giant leap forward not only in computer technology, but people technology as well.

As you proceed through this book, you will see this amazing machine sliced in tasty morsels. And, like the designers of Cupertino, you will catch the excitement and the magic.

The First Slice:

The MacHardware

THE FIRST CHAPTER

The MacCore

You'll Like What You See

Meet Macintosh, the newest Apple; a computer unlike any you've seen before. Some elements of its appearance may be familiar—the color of the case matches that of its predecessors, and it does have a keyboard—but this machine is new from the ground up. We guarantee it will surpass your wildest expectations.

At Apple, the most important concern has always been to build computers that behave like people, not cold impersonal machines. Powerful computational tools have little value if they require thirty manuals to figure out and a doctorate in mathematics to operate. Ideally, working with a computer should be like talking to a very bright friend who is eager to help get your work accomplished.

To achieve that quality, the engineers at Apple had to design Macintosh from the outside in. They gave the machine a personality first and then built intelligence behind that human quality. We will talk more about that personality in what is referred to as technical terms in Chapter 2.

Starting at the Skin in

Before we discuss what the machine can do, let's talk about more obvious details. The main unit of Macintosh stands about a foot tall and is approx-

Fig. 1-1 **The unit is taller than it is wide to conserve workspace on a desk. In fact, Macintosh occupies an area as small as a standard sheet of paper.**

imately eight inches wide. It does not dominate a desktop. In fact, it takes up an area the size of a standard sheet of paper (**Fig. 1-1**).

A screen for displaying information is built into Mac. It measures nine inches diagonally (**Fig. 1-2**). Information is shown in black and white on the monitor. (When you learn what Macintosh can do, computers with color displays will seem pretty pale.) What appears on the screen is built from a collection of discrete illuminated dots. There are 512 dots in the horizontal direction and 342 dots in the vertical direction **across** the screen. Underneath the bottom edge of the bezel that surrounds the screen is a small control dial that sets the display intensity at a comfortable level. The screen is angled to prevent glare, and is situated so that you and Mac look eye to eye. If you would like to adjust the viewing height of Mac, its small size makes it easy to bring to a comfortable level.

Beneath and to the right of the screen, a slot takes the diskettes that contain programs for Macintosh. Programs give computers the basic instructions necessary to solve problems and perform useful work. The nature of the information presented to a computer by a program is somewhat like the training people get when they start a new job. The training establishes the general nature of work to be accomplished in the office environment, what special tools are available for problem solving, and how the product of labor is to be arranged. The device within the computer that reads the program information contained on the diskettes and stores the information you want to retain is called a *disk drive.*

Fig. 1-2   Macintosh has a 9-inch screen, an integral microfloppy disk drive that takes 3½ inch disks, a detachable keyboard, and a mouse input device.

A Tiny Disk Drive

The disk drive within Macintosh is quite unusual. Most personal computers use disk drives that accept 5/4-inch floppy disks. Floppy disks are flat, round pieces of plastic that look a little like miniature 45-rpm phonograph records. They are contained within protective jackets but are more flexible, hence floppy. Information is placed on and read from the floppy disks in much the same way a recording tape is made and played back. Unlike your favorite Beatles tape, the information on floppy disks is not one continuous stream but a series of pieces, which are appropriately called bits.

Conventional floppy disks that hold information on one side retain about 240 thousand bytes. The disks that Macintosh uses, called *microfloppy disks,* hold almost twice that amount: 400 thousand bytes. Even though the microfloppy disks hold a lot more information than 5¼-inch disks, they are physically much smaller. The microfloppy disks are only 3½ inches in diameter. Actually, the microfloppy disks are not too floppy at all, compared with their conventional cousins. Instead of a thin protective jacket, the microfloppy disks are enclosed by an inflexible plastic envelope. They are, as a result, less sensitive to damage. You can put one in your shirt pocket (try doing that with a conventional floppy disk) and you don't have to worry about inadvertently scratching it when you put your ballpoint pen away.

Ordinary floppy disk drives have a little door that has to be shut after the disk is inserted. The slot in the front of Macintosh has no door; you just slide in the microfloppy disk. When you and Mac are totally finished with your work, you tell Mac to eject the disk and it pops partially out of the slot for retrieval.

For additional storage, an external microfloppy disk drive is available (**Fig. 1-3**). You will probably want at least one additional drive to maintain files for future reference as well as additional storage capacity. Without the extra drive, Mac retains only approximately 8½ standard-sized pages of single-spaced text on the microfloppy disk that comes with the word-processing and graphics programs from Apple. The disk installed internally on Macintosh is therefore designed to hold the programs which you will use to manipulate information.

A Bit about Bits

Notice, We told you a little about bits; these are the information pieces used by the computer, as they relate to the disk drives. But bits and Mac do more.

The process of using bits to describe something is quite like a game of twenty questions. A series of yes and no statements put together give you the full story. Eight bits of information equals one *byte* (you can, if you want, equate this to a character also) by definition. Macintosh assimilates

Fig. 1-3 **The optional external microfloppy disk drive
retains 840 Kbytes.**

information in groups of 16 bits, and can process two of these words at a
time (32 bits). We can then say that the processor in Mac is a 16-bit microprocessor that can process 32-bit data. This ability to process so many bits
at a time gives Mac most of its power.

To Macintosh, 16 bits of information represent a *word*. Macintosh hears
and considers information on the basis of words to make decisions, rather
than bit by bit. We do pretty much the same thing when we read. Words
convey meaning; letters make up words and of themselves have no particular
import to us. But don't get confused, the word(s) you are reading now and
the word(s) Mac understands are two different things. For example, let's
take the word Mac. It is made up of 3-letters. Each of these letters is represented by 8-bits (a byte), thus we have 24-bits represented in the English
word Mac, throw in one more character and we have all 32-bits represented—
the way Mac can process information best.

Theoretically, you could assume that Mac could handle its own name in
one fell swoop. For all practical purposes, and as far as you're concerned, it
does. However, the word of 32 bits used internal to the computer is special
and contains more than just data about the creation of a letter or symbol.

The MacConnection

The MacEngineers were pretty smart, since they realized that you more
than likely would want to have a keyboard that was just as friendly as the

rest of the machine. So they made it smart and easy to attach. A socket at the bottom right corner of the front panel mates with the cable from the keyboard.

The plug and socket look similar to those that connect telephones to wall outlets (modular jacks). You can put the keyboard on your lap, on the other side of your desk, or situate it right under the screen. The remote keyboard arrangement permits you to work in whatever position you find most comfortable. This can be a real blessing for knowledge workers who are less than fastidious about organizing their desks. With a typewriter, or many other personal computers that have keyboards rigidly attached, papers with information to be copied have to be adjacent to the machine. With Mac, if you run out of room for papers on your desk you can always turn to the floor and move the keyboard and mouse with you (remember: the cords are not miles long so you might want to bring Mac down there too).

And if you are one of those that like numeric keypads, you can attach that too. This is an option since it was felt that most MacUsers would have little need for tabulating numbers quickly, and that the MacMouse would solve most input difficulties (**Fig. 1-4**).

Fig. 1-4   **To enter numbers in a hurry, the numeric keyboard is the answer.**

And on the Back . . .

Other than the keyboard, all connections to Macintosh are located on the rear panel. At the bottom of the panel, from left to right:

- A MacMouse socket
- An optional external MacMicrofloppy disk drive port
- A serial port which can be used for the MacPrinter (Imagewriter)
- And a second serial port which can be used for the MacModem

In addition, above and to the right of that row of sockets is the receptacle for the power cord (**Fig. 1-5**). A rocker switch above the power cord turns Macintosh on and off. A jack next to the four sockets already described provides the connection for audio output.

So that you can keep your Macintosh nailed down, there is a place for an optional security bracket on the left side, that prevents Mac from disappearing mysteriously.

And to keep everything on time, a tiny compartment at the upper right corner of the rear panel holds a battery that runs the time clock kept by Mac.

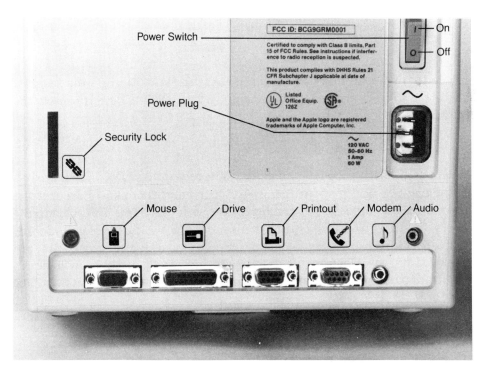

Fig. 1-5   With the exception of the socket at the front for the keyboard cable, all connections are made at the rear panel.

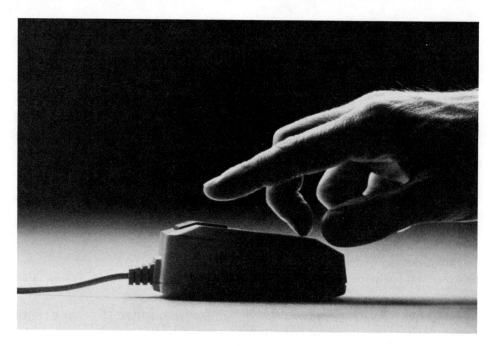

Fig. 1-6 **Instead of keyboard-entered commands, most operations
depend upon pointer selections made by movement of the
mouse. A single button directs entries.**

So that you can move Mac around easily (be sure to undo the security
lock first), there is a handle molded into the top. And believe it or not, the
machine is light and transportable.

It's All Right to Point

We mentioned a socket for a mouse. The *MacMouse* is not a rodent. The
MacMouse is a device about the size of your hand that skates around the
desk when you move it—to communicate with Mac (**Fig. 1-6**). Chapter 3
covers the structure and operation of the mouse, as well as the MacKeyboard,
in detail. Basically, you use the mouse to point to, and select things that are
displayed on the Macintosh screen. Pointing, you'll discover, will be an
important part of your relationship with Mac and is not the least bit impolite.

Getting under the Skin

That about covers what's visible outside Macintosh. Let's check out what's
under the hood (**Fig. 1-7**).

The biggest single item within Mac is the cathode ray tube (*CRT*) that
displays information. The upright board alongside the CRT holds the switching

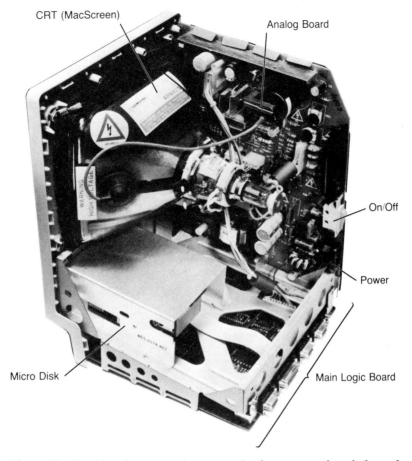

Fig. 1-7 Besides input and output devices, two circuit boards retained in a light stamped frame, a CRT, and the microfloppy drive comprise Macintosh.

power supply that converts the energy from your wall outlet into the proper form to feed Mac's innards.

Incidentally, Mac has a very tolerant appetite, so only really awful foul-ups at utility companies cause hiccups.

In addition to the system power supply, the upright board incorporates circuits to drive the display and generate sound. The switch to turn on Macintosh, and the receptacle for the power cord are soldered to the board as well (**Fig. 1-8**). The correct name for this board, in case you are interested, is the *analog board.*

All logic circuits (the stuff that does the computing) are contained on another board (the *digital board*—in case you're wondering), which is located at the bottom of the MacChassis.

CRT & Power Supply Components

Fly Back Transformer for CRT

On/Off Switch

Line Cord

Speaker

Fig. 1-8 In addition to the system power supply, the card mounted upright within the frame holds the sound generator, and the high-voltage supply for the display.

Something to Wow about

To eyes that have never been bloodshot from reading engineering texts, and from endless tinkering without sleep locked up in design labs, the logic board doesn't look like a big deal. In fact, it is a phenomenal accomplishment (**Fig. 1-9**).

At the center of the board is a *Motorola 68000 microprocessor*, the MacEngine (see Appendix A for more detail on this device). In relative terms, the 68000 chip has the power of a Lamborghini twelve. If you don't know what a Lamborghini twelve is, you're really missing something. Just be aware it's more powerful than a Volkswagen.

At this point, just be aware that the 68000 performs all the decision making within Macintosh.

A Memory That Is Big Enough

Approximately 131 thousand bytes (128-Kbytes) of *dynamic random-access memory (RAM)* is available on the board for the transient storage of information required while the computer is running. (A Kbyte equals 1024 bytes.) Think of this as storage for enough words to make several really excellent mystery novels. The RAM is a holding ground for information during the processing cycle which retains data only while powered. When a microfloppy disk is installed in the MacDrive, the program information on disk is loaded into the RAM. There is really no mystery or big deal of loading information from disk to RAM. Think of the process as being the same as a mail carrier taking letters from his or her bag and putting them into the collection of boxes at an apartment house.

It Never Forgets

Another type of memory—this one permanent—is contained on the logic board also. This memory, called ROM for Read Only Memory, because it cannot be changed—its contents are always there and always the same. The 64 Kbytes (65,536 memory locations) of ROM create the MacPersonality. The contents of the ROM guide the way the 68000 MacEngine makes decisions and establish the manner in which Mac deals with you.

Management of the microfloppy disk drive is performed by another processor on the board that is dedicated especially to that task. The ROM has information in it that controls the disk also, but it relies on other programs that handle the operation in concert with this special processor.

Keeping It on Time and in Line

The shiny oblong device by the Macintosh name on the board is a clock that sets the pace for the 68000. All the operations in the Mac, from the display screen video to the operation of the program that does all of the computation work, are controlled by this clock.

All connections to Macintosh, except for power, are made directly to the logic board. A cable links the digital board to the upright analog card.

A lightweight stamped metal chassis supports all the components in Mac. The plastic enclosure about the assembly is lined with conductive material that prevents radio-frequency energy and other spurious electromag-

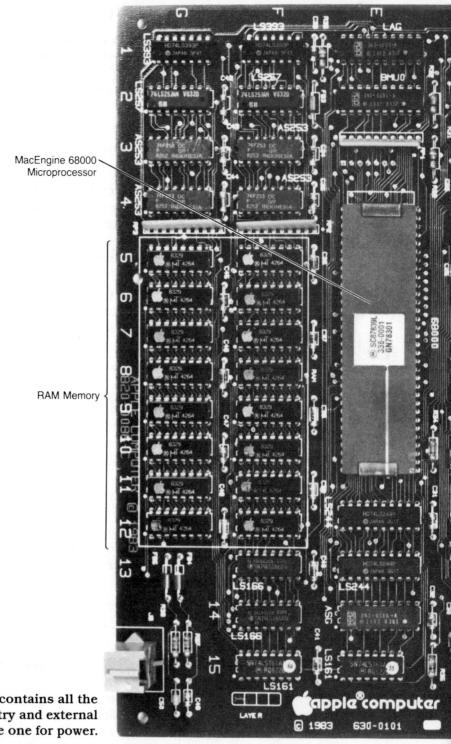

MacEngine 68000
Microprocessor

RAM Memory

Fig. 1-9 **This board contains all the
logic circuitry and external
connectors, save the one for power.**

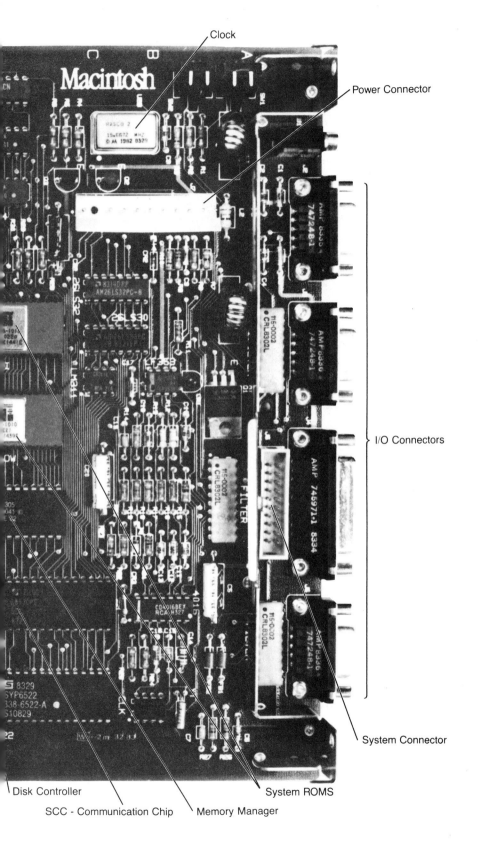

Clock

Power Connector

I/O Connectors

System Connector

Disk Controller

SCC - Communication Chip

Memory Manager

System ROMS

**Fig. 1-10 In total, Macintosh weighs a scant 20 pounds.
A handle is molded into the case.**

netic radiation from fouling up your television reception, opening your garage door, or otherwise altering the normal events in your life. Altogether, Macintosh weighs a scant 20 pounds. And as we said earlier, you can carry it around with a fair amount of ease (**Fig. 1-10**).

Small, Cool and Better

Enormous effort at Apple went into shrinking the size of Macintosh as much as possible—and at the same time to alleviate the need for a fan. Fans are undesirable, of course, because they make noise and consume power. At a point, however, components can be packed too closely together to dissipate heat by convection and a fan is required to prevent a smoking mess.

Interestingly, after tens of thousands of designer work hours were spent paring every conceivable unused cubic inch of space from Macintosh during development, people in Apple marketing got a terrible scare. Focus group meetings set up to determine the opinion of potential buyers revealed something very strange.

The people in the focus groups had never used computers. They were presented with two unmarked machines: the Macintosh, and a bulky, conventional personal computer with about a fifth the power of Mac. When asked to choose which of the computers offered more performance, based on appearance, most of the focus group surveyed indicated that the conventional computer probably was capable of doing more than Mac because it was bigger. The response was a shocker—but wisdom prevailed. Mac is a trim runner in a universe of ungainly sloths.

Some MacHistory

Macintosh was designed to be produced in volume. The system, therefore, had to be as economical as possible. To build Macs Apple constructed a $20 million fully automated assembly facility that was modeled on Japanese factories. When operated at full steam, the plant can produce a Mac every 27 seconds for three shifts a day. At that production rate, the quality of incoming components must be extraordinary. When the resources for the Macintosh project were gathered, reliable sources of virtually defect-free components had to be established. Apple launched one of the industry's most ambitious incentive programs to ensure that parts delivered to Apple were fault free. There are now over 100 companies that are part of the Apple *zero-defects supplier program* that have demonstrated their ability to produce millions of perfect components. Of course, Apple designed and built its own automatic test system for quality control of parts and review of each Macintosh produced at several stages during manufacture.

One consideration during the packaging phase of design was that Mac should fit underneath an airline seat. It does, comfortably. We know, since in the writing of this book it was necessary to travel between Palo Alto and Los Angeles, and keep close tabs on the machine at all times.

A fabric carrying case is available for Mac with compartments for disks, mouse, and keyboard (**Fig. 1-11**). The carrying case has a shoulder strap and handle. You might think that it's silly to carry around a Macintosh, but this is no different than other artists carrying their tools. And frankly, Mac turns everyone into an artist.

Turn It into Paper

For hard copies (printed on paper) of your work, you'll need a Mac-Printer. One is available from Apple. This printer, called the *Imagewriter*, prints everything that you see on the screen. While the Imagewriter (**Fig. 1-12**) from Apple is the first printer to print the graphics of Mac, others will soon be available from third party vendors.

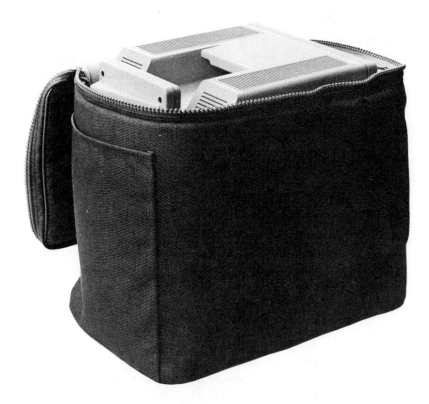

Fig. 1-11 Pouches within the fabric carrying case hold the mouse keyboard, cables, and diskettes. The case has a shoulder strap and fits beneath an airline seat.

The Imagewriter is a wire-matrix impact printer that has a resolution fine enough to render crisp duplicates of whatever appears on the Macintosh screen.

This ability to produce fine line graphics (called bit or raster graphics) is due to special programs in ROM located in the printer. These programs recognize commands from Mac and perform the necessary functions. An exciting aspect of this capability is that you can create just about anything you want in terms of graphics output.

If art is your thing, Mac can do art for you. You can create artwork for a book you are writing—that's how this book was produced (**Fig. 1-13**).

Although Imagewriter is pretty capable, in the near future Apple will offer a laser printer for even better hard copies of the graphics on your screen—produced faster than the currently available impact printer. This is the ultimate in technology—laser printers offer such fine resolution this book could be printed on it with clarity equal to an offset press. Moreover, it can be printed as quickly. So you see, more is still in the wings.

Fig. 1-12 Anything manufactured on the screen can be reproduced by the wire-matrix printer.

There Is Still More . . .

Now that you know something of the Mac system hardware, let's forge ahead with a closer examination of the two input devices that are used to enter information.

Fig. 1-13   Complex artwork is Mac's forte.

THE SECOND CHAPTER

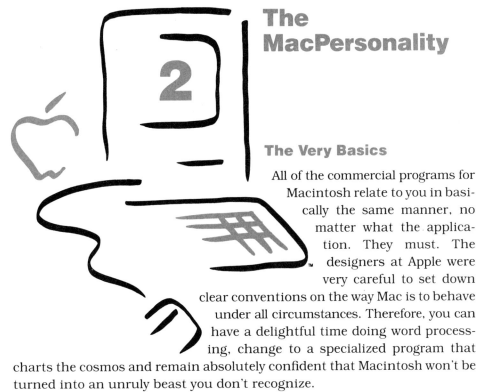

The MacPersonality

The Very Basics

All of the commercial programs for Macintosh relate to you in basically the same manner, no matter what the application. They must. The designers at Apple were very careful to set down clear conventions on the way Mac is to behave under all circumstances. Therefore, you can have a delightful time doing word processing, change to a specialized program that charts the cosmos and remain absolutely confident that Macintosh won't be turned into an unruly beast you don't recognize.

The Macintosh design philosophy holds that people who have no computer experience should be able to perform tasks common to the office and home by applying familiar tools—to that end, graphics should be used to represent those environments, rather than alphanumeric abstractions. As much as possible, all commands and data should be represented by graphics, as well as any other features of the application program.

To sum up what the designers had in mind for Macintosh at the outset:

- Macintosh should approach all tasks in a consistent manner.
- Graphic representations of familiar objects should be employed in application programs whenever possible to characterize procedures and results.

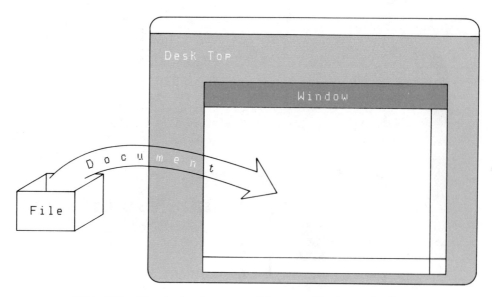

Fig. 2-1   **Moving a document from a file to a window.**

These two statements set the way Mac interfaces with you no matter what tasks the two of you perform. The theme of the user interface conventions is founded on conceptual models.

The Desktop

Consider the Macintosh screen as a flat work surface with the physical qualities of a *desktop*. File folders and documents can be put anywhere on the desktop (**Fig. 2-1**), then moved to make room for others of immediate interest or stacked according to whim. There is absolute latitude to be compulsive about order or as free as the breeze in arranging what you keep on the desktop.

Stale files can be dragged to a wastepaper basket, then retrieved on second thought, or emptied with the trash (**Fig. 2-2**). A notepad, scrapbook, calculator and other accessories can be on the Mac desktop too.

To meet the user interface stipulations set down by the Mac designers, all application programs, no matter what company writes them, must present a metaphor for the working environment of the application that is based on the notion of a flat, oblong work space.

The Finder

The *Finder* is a built-in application program for organizing and managing your documents. When you first start Mac and when you are moving from one application to another, you are using the Finder. We can then say

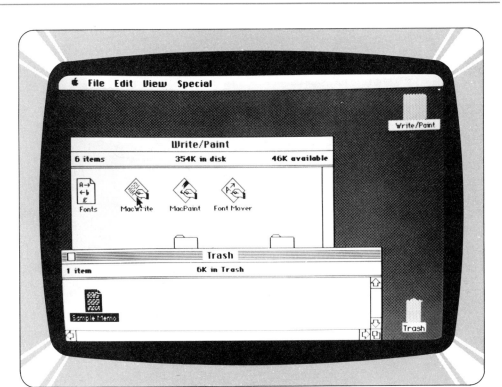

Fig. 2-2   **To discard a file, it is symbolically dragged to a trash basket.**

that the Finder is used to help you find and select the proper application and documents.

The Finder is used to:

- Copy documents
- Rename documents
- Remove documents
- Start applications
- Get documents
- And to put documents away

Every file has a *type* signifying its nature (what it's used for), a *size* of its contents; a *name* it can be called up by; and a *label* for comments. In addition, files carry the *date of creation* and *last modification*.

Working Hard with MacApplications

Application programs are can be thought of as tools to manipulate information.The first available application programs from Apple, MacPaint and

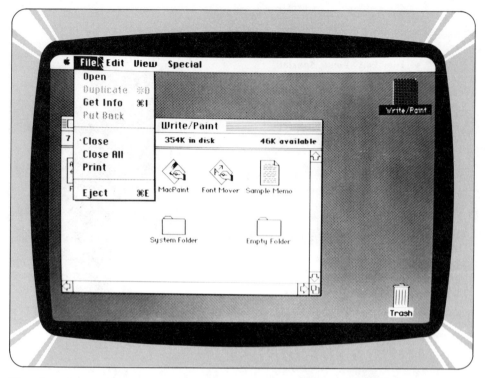

Fig. 2-3 All software for Macintosh creates a list of menus at the top of the screen. A menu can be pulled down by the pointer.

MacWrite, facilitate the creation and editing of graphics and text. Any MacApplication manifests itself in two ways: it displays a *menu bar* at the top of the MacScreen, which in turn lists *menus of commands;* and it places a *document window* on the desktop, through which you can view the information contained within a file (**Fig. 2-3**).

An *application* is an abstraction—with lists of procedures and data structures—deciphered by the computer to accomplish tasks. An application resides within a file. To use an application, you can select a document which uses that application or simply select the application. We can then say that a document contains information as to the nature of the application connected with it. Documents therefore are modified with the application— you cannot, however, alter the contents of an application.

Peeking through the MacWindows

Windows display information. They look like two-dimensional opaque plates, which can be varied in size and shape. Windows appear to float in space above the desktop surface on the MacScreen. Each window floats in a plane by itself, so windows can overlap. Windows can be superimposed in any order but only the window on top is active (that is, can accept alterations to the material it displays).

As each window is created, as you will find in Chapter 4, it takes *precedence* over others on the screen to become active. However, if you decide that a window that is under the new one should be called up for review, you can bring it to the forefront for alteration and it becomes active.

To *scroll text* within a window, bars are provided on the bottom and right-hand sides of the window. The *scroll bars* are capped on each end by boxes that contain arrows. The arrows within the boxes on each scroll bar point in opposite directions. When clicked into activity by the pointer, an arrow scrolls the text in the direction the arrow points. Text can be scrolled line by line or moved continuously.

Multiple windows each representing part of the same logical document can be displayed simultaneously by some tools. The windows can represent different parts of one text, such as the beginning and end of a long essay. Alternatively, multiple windows can permit several documents to be viewed and edited simultaneously. Each tool can manifest a unique philosophy to justify multiple windows as part of its program functions.

The initial position of a window is set by constraints within the tool used. To uncover overlapped windows or make more room on the desktop, windows can be moved.

Documents Are Information

A *Document* is defined as a set of information that the user has created or wishes to alter. Files on microfloppy disks hold documents and documents can reside within the MacMemory.

Most documents contain just one type of information; all text or diagrams, for example. However, information of one type can be added to a document of a different type. In that case, the file retains its original complexion and only the information within that category can be manipulated. An example of this would be a page in a book. A typical page is composed of both text and pictures. The MacPaint program can prepare illustrations or pictures for the page. The MacWrite program would be used to compose the text and would use a picture prepared by MacPaint. It is important to note that once the picture is stored within the document maintained by MacWrite, it can no longer be manipulated by the MacPaint program. The picture which was "pulled in" by MacWrite can still be manipulated in its original form by MacPaint, and the updated picture could be inserted into the MacWrite document in place of the old one.

Each kind of document is associated with a principal tool: the one most likely to manipulate it. The principal tool for any document is usually the one that created the document. In some cases, other tools can read and interpret information on a document.

Three main types of documents are defined according to their structure. They can broadly be classified as files for documents (*texts*), pictures (*free-form*) and arrays of data (*structured*).

Texts consist of a string of linearly ordered information. Information elements can be inserted at any point on the string.

Free-form documents, unlike texts, have no order among their constituent elements. They start empty and unstructured, like a blank piece of paper. Information can appear in any area of such documents but each piece of information occupies its own position. Pictures formed by a graphics editor appear in free-form documents.

Structured documents contain information in predefined cells. Spreadsheet programs, for example, create structured documents. The number of cells in a structured document is fixed. None can be added or removed. The cells are usually arranged in rows and columns. A given cell resides in one row and one column.

The document type determines the manner in which you select information within a document. For example, information within texts can be selected character by character but information within a structured document is selected cell by cell.

For convenience, documents can have intrinsic graphic structures, such as grids. Those structures usually cannot be rearranged or removed.

You Control the System

The conceptual models discussed are the underpinnings of Macintosh programs from any author. Another set of accords establishes standard controls that Macintosh users apply to manipulate information in any program setting.

A simple paradigm governs all dialog between the user and Macintosh: first select some information, then manipulate it. You always have the latitude to select the information to be addressed without being committed to a set of consequent operations, under the terms of the paradigm.

There are three conventional control mechanisms available for any Macintosh application programmer to apply: *buttons*, *check boxes* and *dials*. All three are graphic inventions that respond to a pointer moved into place by the mouse.

Buttons usually appear in a window (although they can be located on the desktop) and are labeled with words or icons. When clicked, buttons can sometimes perform a quick action. When pressed, some buttons perform a sustained action. The action performed is dependent on the button's label. Most of the time, buttons set off quick actions.

Check boxes display a state that you can change. In a group, they represent a check list. Check boxes typically are placed next to a label or icon for definition. Clicking in a check box flips its state from checked to unchecked and vice versa. Alternatively, a selection of check boxes can be arranged so that only one choice can be made. In that case, the appearance of a box is distinct from that of ungrouped check boxes.

Dials show the value or position of properties within a work environment or the system, and can permit you to adjust values. The scroll bar for windows is a good example of a dial. The indicator of the scroll box (also known as a scroll bar) represents the position of the window over the length of the document. To change the position of the window, you can move the indicator by dragging the pointer.

Find It When You Need It

A *selection* is defined as a collection of information that will be acted on by the next command. Just one active selection exists at any time within an active window. The selection can include all the information in the displayed document or can be limited to a single piece of information. When the scope of a selection is confined to one piece of information within a document, the selection is called an *insertion point*. An insertion point indicates the position at which new entries to the document will be placed.

By convention, *clicking a pointer* selects one piece of information or a position between pieces of information. *Dragging a pointer* selects a group of information. The specific effect of clicking and dragging depend on the structure of a document as well as the application.

Clicking in the text selects the position between the two characters nearest the pointer—the insertion point. The insertion point within text is marked by a blinking vertical bar.

Clicking in a structured document selects either the cell beneath the pointer, the position between two adjacent cells, or the corner of four cells. The latter two selections are insertion points and are represented by blinking vertical or horizontal bars.

Clicking in a free-form document selects the item under the pointer. If the pointer is not over information, clicking does nothing or simply selects an insertion point.

Within any editable document, clicking always creates a new selection. Information selected becomes highlighted and the previous selection returns to normal. Highlighted text appears white on a black background.

The Best Kind of Dragging

Dragging a pointer through editable information selects a cluster of information, from the point the mouse button is pressed to the point at which the button is released. Items at the two points are selected, as well as all items between.

Dragging through text selects all characters in order, from the character at the start point, to the character at the end point. Dragging through a structured document selects all cells at the start point, to the cell at the end point. Dragging a pointer through a free-form document selects all items completely enclosed by the start and end points.

As a pointer is dragged, information is highlighted according to the position of the pointer. However, the information is not actually selected until the mouse button is released.

If a pointer is dragged beyond a window's border, the contents of the window continue to scroll away from that border. New information scrolled into the window becomes selected and is highlighted accordingly. Scrolling stops when you either release the mouse button or move the pointer back into the window.

Commands to Keep Order

Once the information to be operated on has been selected, you have to designate how the information is to be manipulated. A Macintosh *application* (also known loosely as a *tool*) displays a bar at the top of the screen which is used for the menu.

The entries in the menu bar and the corresponding menus are different for each tool. However, the entries in the menu bar and the corresponding menus remain constant for a particular tool in all instances of its use.

To gain access to a menu, the mouse is used to position the pointer in the desired title listed in the menu bar. To view the menu, you hold down the button on the mouse while the pointer is in the menu title. The menu descends from the menu bar and remains on the screen until the mouse button is released or the pointer is moved from the menu.

Each item in the menu indicates an operation that can be performed on the information selected. Items in the menu are generally combinations of icons and words. To invoke a command that is represented by one of the items, you drag the pointer down the menu to the desired item and release the mouse button (**Fig. 2-4**). As soon as the button is released, the item blinks briefly, the menu disappears, and the command is executed. The menu title in the menu bar remains highlighted until the command execution is complete.

A command is executed only if the mouse button is released when the pointer is over an item in the menu. Opening a menu from the menu bar *does not* commit you to invoke a command.

Given the rule that the menu bar and menu listings remain consistent under all circumstances within a particular tool, sometimes some menu items will not be applicable. When menu items are irrelevant, they look different than valid items in the menu. Irrelevant items appear gray and indis-

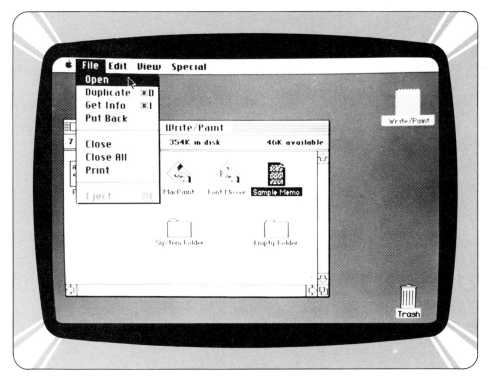

Fig. 2-4 Selecting an item from a menu simply involves pointing and then releasing the mouse button.

tinct. Even if all the items in a menu are irrelevant at a particular time, that menu can still be viewed. In such a case, that menu's title appears gray to set it apart from the titles of active menus along the menu bar.

Commands that can be invoked from the keyboard show the command-key symbol and the appropriate letter in the menu.

Some Menus Are Standard

Although every application (tool) has its own menus of commands, standard menus are always included as well. The commands within the standard menus cover functions that pertain to all Macintosh programs: inquiring the state of the current tool and data; invoking global system functions; editing; and *loading, saving,* and *printing documents.*

The Apple Is Very Special

The *Apple symbol* (logo) on the left end of the menu bar heads a menu that lists accessories for the desk (**Fig. 2-5**). These accessories are the common things you would find on an ordinary desk, such as a calculator. The

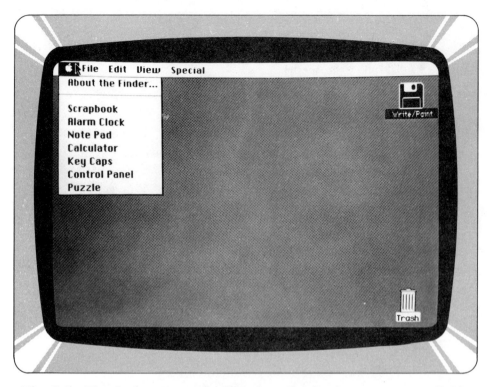

Fig. 2-5 **The desk accessories listed on the Apple menu are available to help you at any time.**

list of standard desk accessories changed during the development of Macintosh. At the time this chapter was written, seven desk accessories were incorporated within the system software.

With most applications, the accessories can be called up for use while work on a document is in progress. When active, the accessories overlay documents. When inactive, they can be obscured by documents or set aside on a clear area of the desktop. Information can be taken from the desk accessories, transported, and pasted into documents. In some cases, information can be lifted from documents and fit within the desk accessories.

When Numbers Are Needed

A calculator can be called from the list (**Fig. 2-6**). It looks like a real four function calculator. The keys on the instrument can be pushed to make entries for calculations by using the mouse to position the pointer over the right key and clicking the mouse button. Alternatively, numbers can be entered from the keyboard or from the optional numeric keypad. The asterisk symbol designates multiplication and the slash symbol designates division. Entries appear on the calculator display. The results of calculations

Fig. 2-6 **The calculator desk accessory performs all the functions of a genuine instrument, but it can't be misplaced.**

can be copied and pasted into documents or other desk accessories. Numbers can be copied from documents and pasted into the calculator's display.

A clock is the next accessory on the menu (**Fig. 2-7**). It shows the current time and date. A replaceable battery at the back of Macintosh runs the clock when the computer is not powered. Just as the results from the calculator can be transported and added to documents, so can the time and date be moved from the clock. You can use the clock to put a "*time-and-date stamp*" on documents.

To set the clock, the appropriate digits can be clicked in from the mouse button. Unless the computer is moved across time zones, the clock needs to be set only when the battery is replaced.

The key caps accessory follows the clock on the menu. An image of the keyboard appears on the desktop in response to the command (**Fig. 2-8**). There is a display at the top of the imaginary keyboard that shows characters typed from the real keyboard or those entered by the mouse in the same way calculator entries are made. Passages from documents can be pasted into the display as well.

The keyboard image indicates all the characters available within the

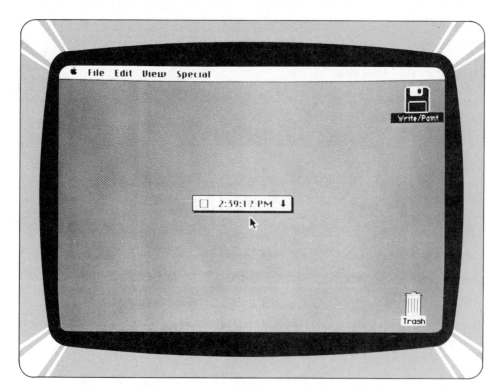

Fig. 2-7   No need to look from your work to a clock on the wall.
Macintosh will give you the time of day.

system. There are many more available characters than keys. When the SHIFT,
CAPS LOCK, or OPTION key is pressed on the real keyboard, the desk accessory image shows the corresponding alternative character sets called up by
the action.

All Work and No Play . . .

A *puzzle* pops onto the screen when the next command from the menu
is selected (Fig. 2-9). Daydreamers can spend hours putting the numbers in
the puzzle in order while application documents gather dust on the desktop.

Down a rung from the puzzle command in the menu is the note pad
command. The pad that appears on the screen when the item is selected
has eight pages available for notes to be set aside from applications. Notes
can be revised by regular editing actions and are automatically saved.

I Remember When

The scrapbook accessory keeps pictures and text for frequent use in
documents. Scroll bars move the contents of the scrapbook for viewing.

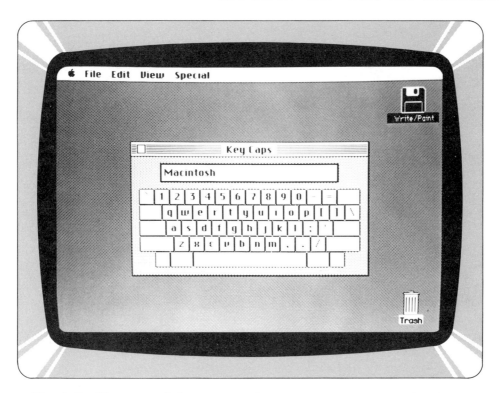

Fig. 2-8   The normal, lower case character set appears ordinarily on
the key caps image.

The last, but probably most visually arresting desk accessory on the list
is the system control panel (**Fig. 2-10**). With it, many characteristics of Mac
can be arranged to suit individual taste. For example, the volume of the tone
generator can be increased or decreased; the pointer (I beam) flash rate can
be changed; and the rate at which the pointer is displaced on the screen
relative to the motion of the mouse can be adjusted.

The Edit Menu

The *Edit menu* includes all the commands necessary to manipulate pieces
of documents (**Fig. 2-11**). Commands on the menu in common to all programs include *UNDO, COPY, CUT, PASTE,* and *SELECT ALL.* Theese commands support the insertion, deletion, and replacement of text, graphics,
and numbers. With them, material can be moved from one area to another
within a document, and from one document to another. An important window is associated with the Edit menu: the *Clipboard window.* The Clipboard holds whatever was last cut or copied from a document. Whatever is
in the Clipboard remains there even when one program is substituted for
another.

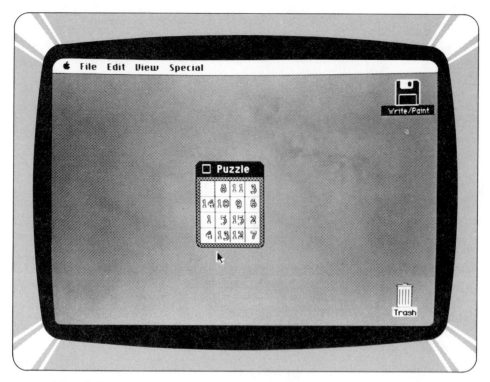

Fig. 2-9 Busy executives like you need a chance to unwind.
Macintosh understands.

Every time a CUT or COPY ccommand is issued, a copy of selected material replaces whatever was lodged in the Clipboard proviously. The *CUT* command allows selected material to be deleted altogether from a document. The *COPY* command puts a copy of selected material into the Clipboard without altering the document at all. The *PASTE* command is pretty much the opposite of CUT. It replaces a selected area of a document with the contents of the Clipboard. When the PASTE command is used, the contents of the Clipboard are not altered. In fact, the command can be used repeatedly to copy and recopy material from the Clipboard to a document.

The *UNDO* command reverses the effect of whatever command was just performed. If the previous operation was an undo, then the command restores the change made by the original command.

Another Tasty Menu

The *File menu* incorporates commands that permit you to open old files and establish new ones, save documents, print documents, and quit the current document. The *QUIT* provision in the File menu ensures that you are aware of the opportunity to save work before leaving it.

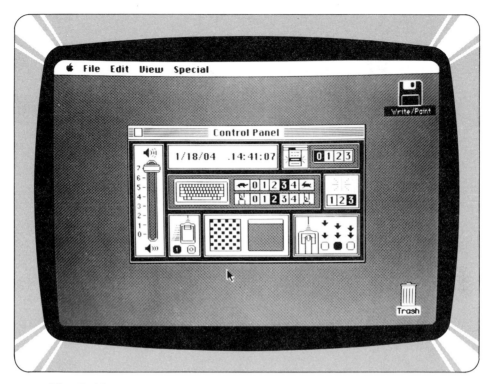

Fig. 2-10 Many characteristics of Macintosh can be adjusted by the control panel.

All commands share some basic properties. First of all, when invoked, they direct an immediate operation. When the operation is complete, control is returned to you—right away. Commands always operate on something visible within the active window, or they add or remove a window on the desktop, or they operate on the active window itself.

Occasionally, a command may require amplification for an appropriate operation to be selected. For example, if the *PRINT* command is selected, Mac needs more information in order to perform a print operation. How many copies must be printed? What size are the printed sheets to be? To clue Mac in to what's on your mind in such a situation, another device is available within the conventions of the Mac user interface. The device is known as a *dialog box*. A dialog box is presented as a rectangle that can contain text, buttons, dials, and other graphic symbols. It is labeled with the name of the command with which it is associated. A dialog box usually incorporates its own menu from which you select information that specifies precisely what the command you selected must accomplish. Two buttons are always included within dialog boxes: *OK* and *Cancel*. The *OK* button affirms the choices made within the dialog box and removes the box from

Fig. 2-11 **There is always an Edit menu within a program.**

the MacScreen. The *Cancel* button dismisses the dialog box without putting any changes into play. In some cases the dialog box may incorporate additional options.

This Is an Alert!

If you transgress the limits of prudent behavior when dealing with Mac, you will be made aware of your improprieties by the appearance of *alert boxes*. Alert boxes are similar in appearance to dialog boxes. Alert boxes provide warnings and indicate errors. The mechanics of alert boxes can vary to reflect the severity of your mistake or the potential for doom. A beep tone is usually emitted from Mac concurrent with the appearance of the alert box.

Mac Maintains Character

Whatever program you use, Mac will interact with you by applying the metaphors discussed. Rest assured that you will be dealing with a cooperative, predictable friend. You may be wondering how all commercial programs for Mac, whether they're written in Palo Alto, California or in Nutley, New Jersey, can possibly employ the same graphic metaphors and relate to you in a fashion consistent with the Macintosh character. The answer is carried within two ROM chips (firmware) inside Mac.

THE THIRD CHAPTER

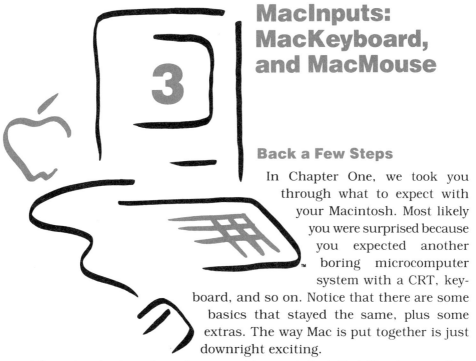

MacInputs: MacKeyboard, and MacMouse

Back a Few Steps

In Chapter One, we took you through what to expect with your Macintosh. Most likely you were surprised because you expected another boring microcomputer system with a CRT, keyboard, and so on. Notice that there are some basics that stayed the same, plus some extras. The way Mac is put together is just downright exciting.

There is a keyboard, and you would expect that. But Mac has another input device called a mouse. We like to refer to this as MacMouse. Because you are more familiar with a keyboard than a mouse, We're going to explain the keyboard first—that way you will be able to really appreciate the importance of both, and how they work together.

Quite Simply the Keyboard

Apple chose to make Mac's keyboard a functional device to enhance your ability to enter information. As you would expect, the keyboard (**Fig. 3-1**) has 58 keys, six of which are defined for special functions. The majority of the keys are arranged in the order that keys appear on an ordinary typewriter. There is a European version of the keyboard also available for Mac, but we will restrict our discussion to the U.S. version only.

Command Key

Fig. 3-1. In all, 256 different characters can be entered from the keyboard. Note the OPTION, ENTER, and BACKSPACE and command keys.

By function, the keys can be divided into three sets: *character keys*, *modifier keys*, and *special keys*. Character keys enter characters into the computer. Modifier keys, in conjunction with character keys, make the selection of different characters on a key. The special keys give special instructions to Macintosh.

The *alphanumeric*, *numeric*, and *symbolic keys*, as well as the space bar, feed Mac characters. Any character key can be associated with more than one character. The modifier keys select the different characters on a key.

The keyboard hardware scans the character keys such that Mac can recognize any two pressed simultaneously. This feature is called two-key rollover.

A Quick Change of Character

Six keys—two that are labeled *SHIFT* on each side of the keyboard, two labeled *OPTION*, one labeled *CAPS LOCK*, and a *command key* (appears as a key with a square and loops on all four corners (a square four leaf clover))—change the interpretation of keystrokes or other inputs to the computer. When one of these keys is held down, the behavior of the other keys (and occasionally that of the mouse button) can change.

The *SHIFT* and *OPTION* keys designate different characters on each character key. The SHIFT keys select the upper character indicated on the top row of keys and uppercase letters. The OPTION key alters the character set for foreign characters and special symbols (**Fig. 3-2**). The SHIFT and OPTION keys can be used together.

The *CAPS LOCK* key latches when pressed once and releases when pressed again. When latched, it makes all lower-case keys emit upper-case char-

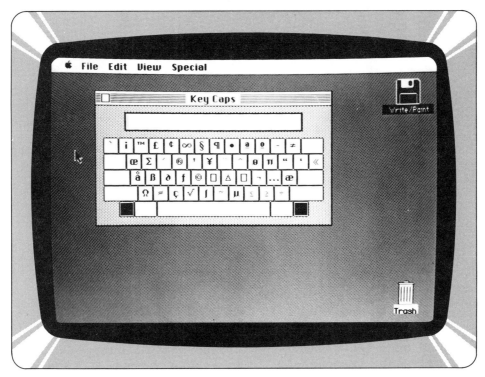

Fig. 3-2 The OPTION key is pressed on the keyboard when the key caps desk accessory is visible; the image reflects the new character set made available.

acters. The CAPS LOCK key has no effect on keys other than letters. It can be used in combination with the OPTION key.

The keyboard hardware can sense any or all of the modifier keys pressed simultaneously, thus allowing for the creation of MacSpecific commands.

When the *ENTER* key is pressed, Mac validates the current entry and admits the next. While this is generally true, in the case of a dialog/alert box it may have the same effect as clicking OK—it will not go on to the next entry—only TAB does that. We can then say that the *TAB* key is applied to signal movement to the next item in a sequence. The *BACKSPACE* key deletes characters from text during the course of typing.

A Mouse in the Computer

As we've been explaining all along, the basis of Mac is to improve productivity. And one of the methods that was chosen to do this is to use a mechanical mouse (a pointing device) to enhance your ability to move around the electronic desktop which Apple created.

The MacMouse (**Fig. 3-3**) is a single-button unit that moves the pointer on the screen as it is moved along a flat surface. The mouse resolves 200

Fig. 3-3 There are three ways by which the button is used to characterize the mouse input: clicking once; clicking twice; and sustained engagement.

Fig. 3-4 At the bottom of the mouse is a ball that rides freely along the surface of a desk.

points per inch of travel, and when at rest, does not disturb the positioning of the screen pointer.

It Rolls Along

Keeping the MacMouse on track is a ball arrangement (**Fig. 3-4**). There are mice and then there are mice. Whereas cousins of the MacMouse use steel ball bearings, and in some cases even wheels to translate motion, the MacMouse incorporates a textured rubber ball (with a metal core) that floats in the housing. The textured rubber ball provides much more friction with the surfaces the MacMouse scampers across.

Other mice must be used on special surfaces marked with grids to describe position. Those mice track the grid markings optically. The MacMouse is not tied to any surface and can be picked up and moved without altering the pointer position. Should room about the computer be tight, you can pick up the MacMouse and roll it along your palm. The ball need only roll a certain distance to displace the pointer a commensurate amount on the screen.

It Clicks and Drags

The mouse not only serves to point, but can be used as a selection and moving device as well. The three mouse actions used to direct Mac are *clicking*, *pressing*, and *dragging*. Clicking entails positioning the pointer with mouse motion, then briefly pressing and releasing the mouse button without moving the mouse. Pressing involves positioning the pointer with the mouse, then pressing and holding the button without moving the mouse. Dragging entails positioning the pointer, then pressing while simultaneously moving the mouse. Clicking something with the mouse performs an immediate action—in other cases it can undo a previous selection click.

Pressing while the pointer is on an object on the screen, usually has the same effect as repeated clicking. For example, clicking a scroll arrow on a window causes a document to scroll one line; pressing a scroll arrow causes the document to scroll continuously until the mouse button is released. Dragging can have various effects, depending on what is under the pointer when the button is pressed. Beginning a drag within a document frequently results in the selection of data. Beginning a drag with the pointer over an object on the screen moves the object. Dragging is also used to pull down a menu from the titles in the menu bar.

Remember the Mouse Words

Since using a mouse may be foreign to you, it's possible that some of the words used to describe its operation may also be. Therefore, we'll summarize the various words that you will find in later chapters of this book and subsequent Sams' books and Apple documentation.

- Mouse button
- Clicking
- Dragging
- Pressing
- Pointer

Hardware and Software

The Macintosh and the Lisa are both designed to use only one *character set* for all the countries that use English and Latin type characters. This character set, **Table 3-1**, contains all the necessary alphanumeric and mathematical symbols that are necessary in any of these countries. As shown in **Fig. 3-5**, the layout is all that really changes to reflect the method of use in those countries.

The character set defines the one-byte codes that internally represent each character. Thus all the Macintoshes, in all the countries, use the same

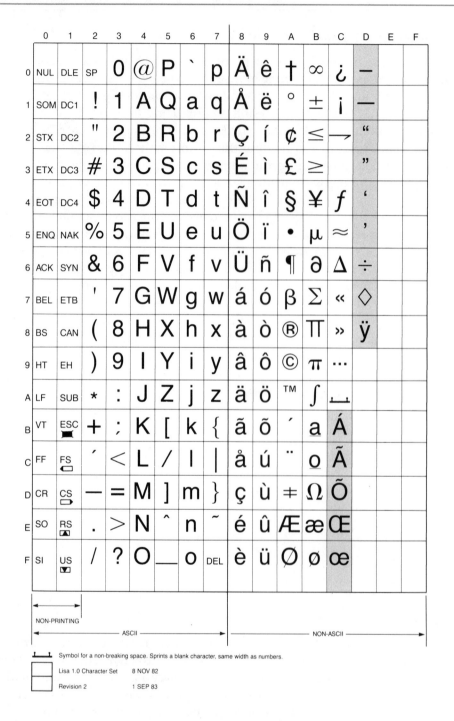

Table 3-1 **Macintosh character set.**

US Keyboard Layout

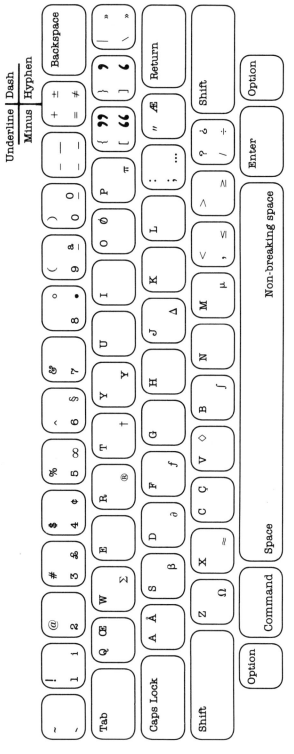

Fig. 3-5 Only the keyboard layout changes from country to country.

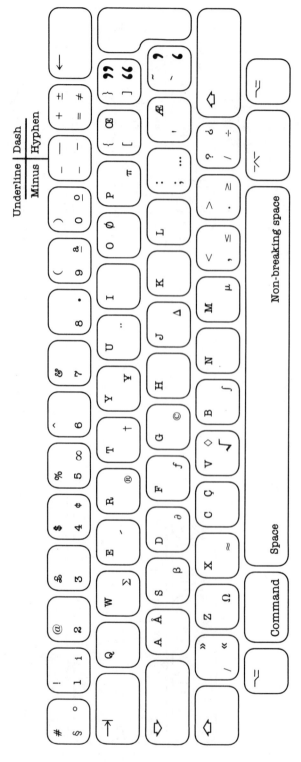

UK Keyboard Layout

Fig. 3-5—(cont.)   Only the keyboard layout changes from country to country.

German Keyboard Layout

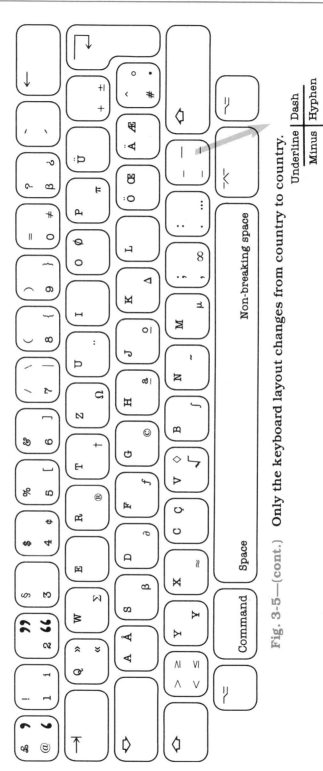

Fig. 3-5—(cont.) Only the keyboard layout changes from country to country.

Spanish/Latin American Keyboard Layout

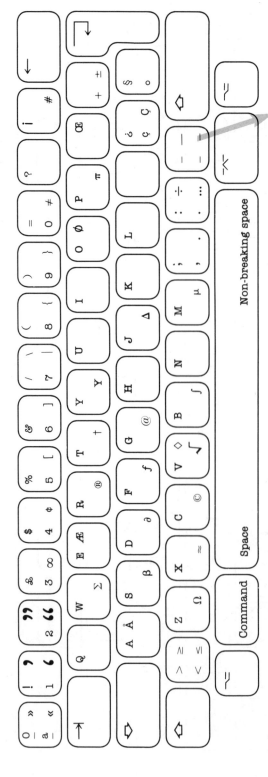

Fig. 3-5—(cont.) Only the keyboard layout changes from country to country.

Underline	Dash
Minus	Hyphen

French Keyboard Layout

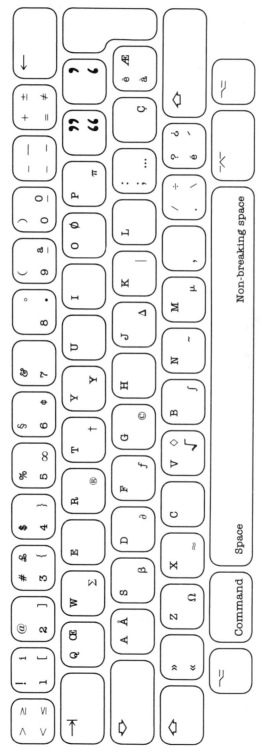

Fig. 3-5—(cont.)   Only the keyboard layout changes from country to country.

French/Canadian Keyboard Layout

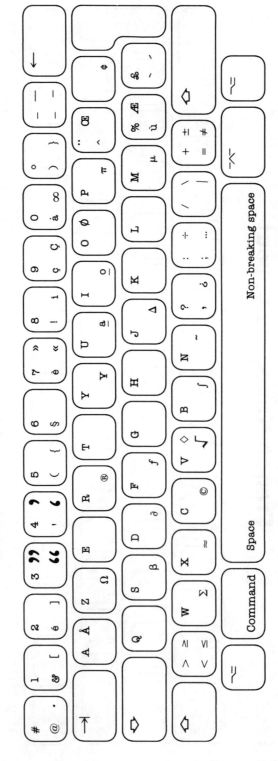

Fig. 3-5—(cont.) Only the keyboard layout changes from country to country.

Italian Keyboard Layout

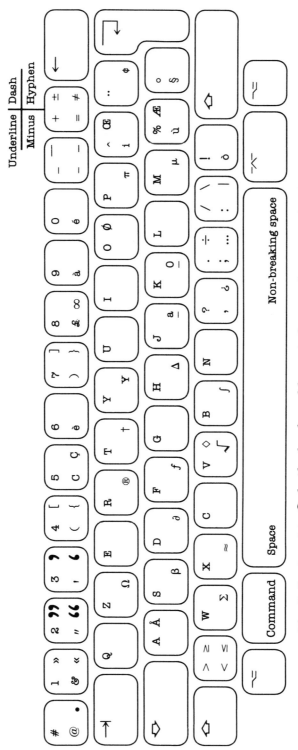

Fig. 3-5—(cont.) Only the keyboard layout changes from country to country.

internal code for all the characters. Unlike other systems that use various bit patterns to define special attributes for each international character set, all the bits are used by Macintosh to define a character, and it never varies.

The characters are defined by a system of fonts that are made up of bit patterns that define specific shapes on the display screen. The font definitions are maintained in a special section of the system that is called on when Macintosh needs to display a character—number or symbol. Interestingly, although you may not be able to access an international font from your Macintosh, the rudiments of the characters are always there and can be turned on using special programs.

As we explained, the difference between keyboards for various countries is the physical layout of the keys. This is easily discernible by perusing **Table 3-1**, and the keyboards shown in **Fig. 3-5**.

As shown earlier in this chapter, you can use the OPTION key to access the characters not shown on the keyboard. This gives you the ability to change functions of the keyboard, and provides you access to the "hidden" keyboard.

THE FOURTH CHAPTER

Opening the Information Shutter

4

A Very Spiffy Viewport

In the previous three chapters, we've led you through the hardware that makes up the Macintosh and shown you the intricate maze behind the user interface.

The real key to Mac, however, is the use of all this magic in the form of windows.

A *window*, in Mac terms, is a portion of the screen through which you see or view information. In fact, the window is used to open an area on the display screen—through this window you can view part or all of your information.

To put this in more human terms, think of a window in a house. Any house will do. The window is covered with opaque drapery. You can, by opening the drapery, have various viewing window sizes of what's on the other side. For example, if you open the drapery just enough to peek through, your viewing area is relatively limited. The more you open the window, the greater the viewing field, until of course you completely expose the window.

This is the simple concept on which computer windows are based.

By now, however, you are fully aware that there is a great deal more to Mac's windows than just a simple viewing port to your information. But we'll get into that in just a bit.

Worth a Thousand Words

Whoever said "a picture is worth a thousand words" apparently had a Mac in mind. The idea behind Mac is to convey information in terms that people can understand and use—a window presents us with information in a form we can understand.

The window on Mac is made up of many elements and concepts. Referring back to our example of a house window, consider what you really would see. First, when just peeking, you might see nothing but a brown surface; as you open the drapery more, a tree with surrounding lawn and the street behind it are revealed.

The Aspect of It All

There are a number of things which control windows:

- Scroll bars
- Positioning of window
- Changing window size

To use the windows in Mac effectively, we will now explain some of the characteristics that can be controlled by them. While the description of the functioning of these windows may seem bewildering, they are quite simple and straightforward. We will describe the characteristics of windows by explaining the typical make-up of a window (**Fig. 4-1**). In order to move through our data, we need to move our point of view. This change of viewpoint, or the actual moving is referred to as *scrolling* (**Fig. 4-2**). Now, since we have data which may be too wide and too tall for the screen, we need to move in both the horizontal (across) and vertical (up/down) directions. To accomplish this movement through the data, we use the mouse and scroll bars to control the movement. This movement through our data is accomplished by *horizontal* and *vertical scroll* bars. By placing the pointer (which is controlled by the mouse) in one of these bars and then dragging the mouse (moving the mouse with the button down), we can change our point of view.

A very handy feature of Mac is its ability to have multiple windows on the screen at the same time. This ability to put up multiple windows presents a possible problem of windows obscuring each other. To alleviate this condition, Mac allows you to reposition windows. To reposition a window you would use the mouse to drag the window by its *title box* (which is the topmost striped bar at the top of the window) into its new position and then release the button on the mouse.

Since we may not be interested in observing all of the possible data in a window, it is sometimes convenient to change the size of a window. This is accomplished by positioning the pointer in the *size box* located in the

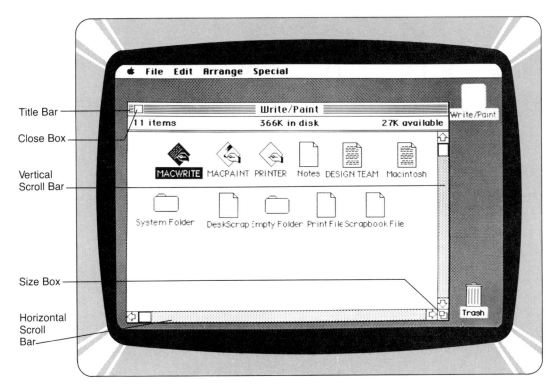

Fig. 4-1 **Anatomy of a window.**

lower right portion of the window and dragging this box to readjust the size of the window.

If you feel a little destructive and would like to remove a window from the screen, you can do this by placing the pointer in the upper left *close box* in the title bar and clicking the mouse (pressing the button momentarily). Removing a window does not mean you have destroyed any information— all you have done is to remove a viewing point of that information.

Windows are devices that Mac uses to allow us to view information on the screen. As you use them, you will discover how easily they are manipulated and act as a convenient display medium.

The Plane Truth

We have examined the use of windows in Mac but what about the actual display of information—how are pictures and text displayed so clearly?

The display screen on which all objects are displayed is composed of a large number of dots. To display an object, the appropriate dots are "turned on" (white dots) while others are "turned off" (black dots). The basic display area of the MacScreen is an array of 512 by 342 dots (175,104 dots), or picture

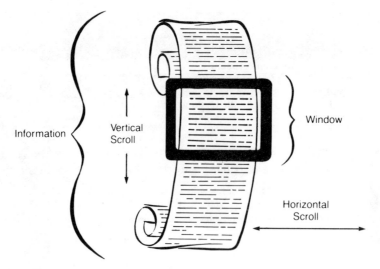

Fig. 4-2 Scrolling.

elements (pixels), arranged on a nine-inch screen. It is the responsibility of the microprocessor in the Mac to control these dots and form images. There are a number of other components that go into defining the resolution capability of a screen, all of them dull. Suffice it to say that the MacScreen is able to display information fine enough to be called a portrait.

To produce such beautiful and detailed graphics, the microprocessor in the Mac has to perform an enormous amount of work. For the moment, consider the number of dots it needs to control. Not only must it know whether to turn any dot on or off, but it has to keep track of its position as well as the position and state of other dots on the screen. The way all of this is performed is to store the information into display memory sections, called planes, that measure 512 x 342. Because the MacEngine (a 68000 microprocessor) is so smart, this is managed using a multiplexing method that swaps information in and out as needed, and overlaps memory areas without losing detail.

The fundamental power of the window method of graphics is to overlay different windows. By clever overlapping, we can see vestiges of windows below the current one being used. Using key information displayed in the vestiges of the covered windows, we can determine what windows are overlapped. We can then say that we can have windows at different levels. The fact that windows overlap without destroying each other (only obscuring) is known as *precedence* or *prioritization*. None of the information being displayed, including *alpha text* (letters, numbers and assorted characters) is flat, or appearing in one level of display memory; rather, it is mapped across all levels. Thus, it is possible to create new windows that overlap old ones and change the dot patterns.

Dots the Emphasis

Since the information associated with the screen is held in memory planes that are brought in and out as needed, the display characteristics can be heightened (**Fig. 4-3**). As shown in this figure, the row of balls appear to have depth and shading. Although not readily apparent in this book due to the very flat nature of the printed page, the balls have an almost three-dimensional appearance when viewed on the MacScreen.

In concept, all that is necessary for you to do to add depth to an object on a CRT screen is to add shading. This shading is accomplished by adjusting the intensity of groups of displayed dots. With a black-and-white-only system, like the Mac, you can control the intensity of an object or an area by varying the density of white and black dots in an area. This effect of shading and depth is enhanced by a process that people in the computer graphics field call *dithering* (randomization). The functional concept of dithering is simple. The mechanisms to do it aren't. With color systems the process is much easier—you vary the intensity of color. Of course we're oversimplifying the process, but you get the idea.

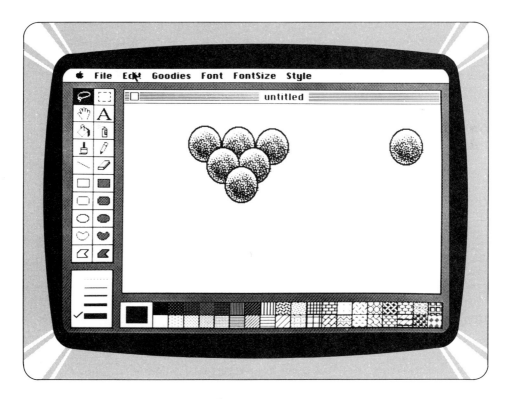

Fig. 4-3 Multiple copies of a figure can be made in a flash on the screen.

Believe it or not, in monochrome (black and white) the process is far more difficult because only two components are allowed: all colors (white) and the absence of color (black). Between black and white there is a range of intensities known as a *gray scale*, which measures how white or black an area is. To control the intensity of an object using black and white dots, we simply turn off the appropriate dots (or pixels). The interesting effect here is that when we turn off dots, rather than simply turning black, they appear to be shades of gray. The more dots we turn off, the darker the area, till we have a significant area of turned-off dots which produces a significant black area. This pseudo-brightness is caused by the adjacent pixels' apparent "lighting" of the adjacent black cell. You can see this effect by examining a black and white picture in a newspaper with a magnifying glass—what you see are black dots with varying spacing. We can do the same thing with Mac—control which dots we wish to turn off, to control the intensity at any point on the screen.

An Automatic Sketch Pad

The method used by Apple with Mac, and of course its big sister Lisa, is to create a screen that is very much like a child's toy sketch pad that has a silver lining that is etched away by the movement of dial-controlled arms.

If you're lucky enough to have a Macintosh, go to the MacPaint program and choose the pencil. Using the MacMouse, begin moving the pencil around. Note very carefully how the pencil is drawing.

Very close inspection would reveal that the line being drawn is by way of removing white information. In fact, what occurs is that dots are being turned off as you move the pencil across the screen—or if you like, changed to black. This is almost like removing frost from a window with your finger.

There is a mode known as *fatbits* which allows you to get a closer look at the pattern of dots close-up. This magnification mode allows you to modify your drawings for very subtle nuances. The best analogy would be that of painting a picture with a miniscule paint brush and an enormous mangifying lens—the result being a very intricate rendering.

More Than One

Now that we know a little about windows and what is contained within them, let's discuss the nature of multiple windows.

Multiple windows represent one of the new fundamental concepts of Mac, which is its ability to allow you to organize your work rather than having to live with the structure of an ordinary program. This concept allows you to put on your screen the information from multiple sources displayed in windows, and then to interchange information between these windows (within some constraints of course).

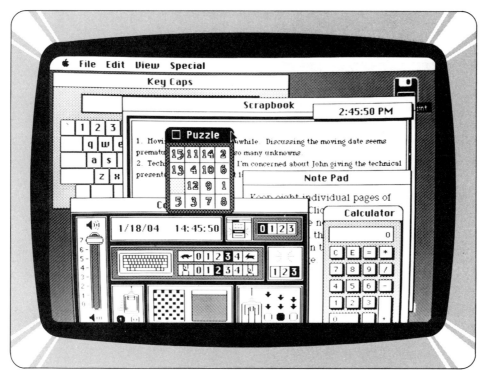

Fig. 4-4 **Many windows can be expanded or reduced as desired. A small box at the lower right-hand corner of windows reacts to the mouse-directed pointer to permit size alterations.**

While more than one window seems like a good idea, we find that the screen is usually smaller than the data available to display. To handle this excess information we can place windows on top of each other. Imagine a stack of folders placed so that you could see both the labels of each of the folders in the stack and the top folder's contents. This is exactly how windows appear. But how then do we look into a folder that is in the stack? The answer is very simple: we just point to the label (or portion of a window) and click the mouse button. The result of clicking an *inactive window* is to make it active while the previously *active window* is made inactive (label or portion visible). As an example, examine **Fig. 4-4.**

As we said, the window or windows present information. You can have single or multiple windows on your screen—called a *desktop*—thus allowing you to view more than one set of information at a time.

Now you know that the windows can be moved, changed in size, scrolled through, or closed, and as we've said, overlapped. Let's next examine how Mac performs this operation by controlling the presentation of information in memory.

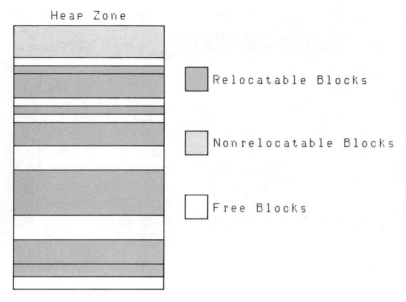

Fig. 4-5   Heap zones are broken up into blocks.

Staying on Top of the Heap

The method used in Macintosh to handle windows and all the other things that go on inside of the machine, is to employ a *memory management chip.* This is a special device that works in tandem with the MacEngine and supervises the display and program methodology. Working in concert with this chip is a program in the ROMs of Mac called the *memory manager* which allocates and controls memory usage. This program combined with special hardware makes Mac very efficient in its handling of memory.

What makes Mac so different, as compared to the first generation of personal computers, is its advanced processor architecture. Unlike these early machines, the 68000 used in the Mac provides for relocation and protection of programs and data. These advanced features account for the incredible performance of Mac. When applied to graphics, this advanced architecture can produce sophisticated graphics in short order. By allocation and deallocation of the available memory in the machine, we make the most effective use of this precious resource.

Memory is allocated to graphics and programs using *heaps.* Each program maintains one or more independent areas of heap memory (Apple calls these *heap zones*), and uses these to allocate blocks of memory of any desired size. You can think of the heap as being an area that is chopped up and used as the needs of the system change (**Fig. 4-5**).

Unlike the space used by the microprocessor called *stack space*, which is allocated and released in a last, in-first-out order, a block within the heap can be released or allocated in any order. This dynamic allocation and deallocation of memory is what accounts for the flexibility in using windows. If it weren't this way, the windows would be too rigid.

There are always two heap zones. One is used by the system and one is maintained for your application. The system heap size is 16 Kbytes during startup and can change dynamically as called for.

The heap zones for the applications such as MacWrite and MacPaint, which you'll learn about later, are reinitialized at the start of the application. Each time the initial size is 6 Kbytes—that's just to get things going. As you begin to use the application, the heap grows either by subdividing the original heap or adding more memory by asking the system for it.

As shown in **Fig. 4-5,** the heap zones are divided into blocks. A byte of information is part of a given block. These blocks contain information about what they are to be used for and their actual contents.

Now you can see how Mac keeps track of the windows and the information in them.

A Block at a Time

A block can be of any size. It is limited only by the size of the heap zone it belongs to. Moreover, the memory management system has no idea, nor does it care, what's inside a block. The memory management system just knows that it is a block of certain size that belongs to a certain heap.

The system maintains a sophisticated system of location items called *pointers* to keep track of where each block is within any given heap, and also to show what the status of a block is. This becomes critical if you plan to write programs for Mac in assembly language, since you have to know what type of block is involved and exactly what you want to do with it. While, strictly speaking, the memory manager will take the proper actions necessary for small programs, you become more involved with the intracies of the allocation of memory as you begin to stretch into large spans of memory.

This effective use of memory by software and hardware accounts for the ability of programs to run quickly in small spaces. In addition to program support, this scheme supports the structure of windows. By effectively providing a well-tuned environment for programs, Mac will allow sophisticated programs to run efficiently.

The Overlapping Concept

The idea behind windows isn't unique to Mac—Apple's Lisa also provides these same (and more) capabilities. Even before Lisa existed, developers at Xerox Palo Alto Research Center (PARC) envisioned a multifunction system whereby information could be shared internally to a machine and externally to a user application. You could think of the machines designed by Xerox PARC as the beginning of the revolution in man-machine interfacing.

Apple has developed the concepts envisioned and demonstrated by the researchers of Xerox PARC into a machine that everyone "already knows how to use." In my opinion, the true beauty of Mac is in its ease of use—it's hard to describe the feeling of finally being able to use a computer without having to read any manuals. This is a machine for people to use—Apple has brought us truly into the age of the *personal computer*—a machine that provides immediate help rather than the need for training.

Apple did, if you will, open the information window to everyone.

The Second Slice:

The MacSoftware

THE FIFTH CHAPTER

The Toolbox · A Quick Draw · Get the Picture
Resource Manager

A MacOverview of Software

5

The Toolbox

To preclude wild shifts in the MacPersonality from program to program, designers at Apple took precautions within the machine to insure that independent suppliers of software won't do anything non-standard. As a result, when you perform some spreadsheet operations with Mac, blissfully you will notice no difference in the machine's general demeanor should you change to vertical software for architectural applications. The nuts and bolts of the provisions to secure Mac melt down to this: to build any kind of reasonable program for Mac, an independent source must employ procedures resident within the machine that maintain its character.

Within the 64 Kbytes of ROM (read only memory) inside Mac, are resources that you and I don't see when we run a program—they form the core of what is known as the *operating system*. The operating system occupies approximately a third of the ROM memory space. The remaining two thirds of ROM is devoted to a collection of various managers and services that save developers years of time, and precious memory space when cooking up a program. Collectively, these managers and services that reside in ROM are known as the *User Interface Toolbox*.

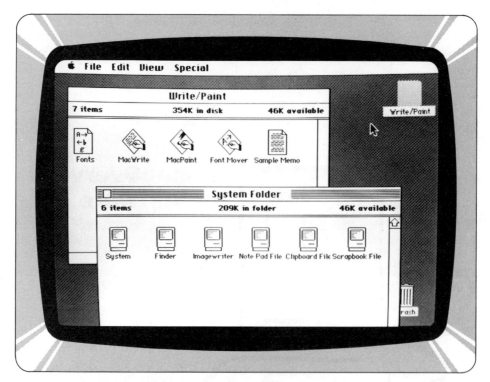

Fig. 5-1 Documents, accessories, and files can occupy the Macintosh desktop in any position or priority.

A Quick Draw

At the heart of the User Interface Toolbox is a revolutionary set of graphics routines called *QuickDraw.* QuickDraw facilitates doing extremely complex graphics operations at animation speeds. QuickDraw treats the Macintosh screen as several independent work areas. Within each area, many things can be drawn. These things can include text, lines, rectangles, ovals and circles, rectangles with rounded edges, wedges, amorphous regions, and angular polygons.

Text can be created in a number of proportionally spaced fonts, with variations that include boldfacing, italicizing, underlining, and outlining. Straight lines can be any length or width. With just one procedural call from the application software, QuickDraw can create a picture made of combinations of these elements.

QuickDraw has the ability to define many distinct graphics ports on the screen, each with its own complete drawing environment. Each port has its own coordinate system, drawing location and character set. An application program would call QuickDraw to switch from one port to another. QuickDraw does not allow the creation of graphics outside appropriate ports. Quick-

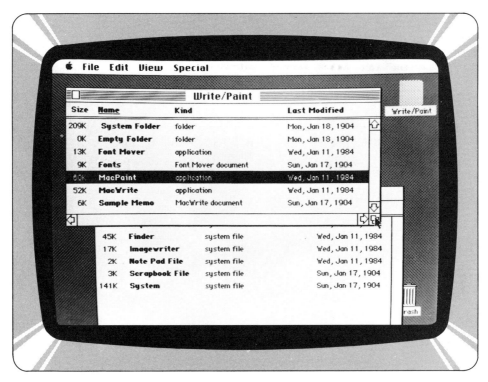

Fig. 5-2. If you don't like icons, you can choose from a list.

Draw can also create drawings off-screen into a buffer as easily as it can manufacture screen graphics. This allows a picture to be forwarded to a printer without any disturbance to screen images.

Get the Picture

If you're still following, let's explore further. QuickDraw is stored within the Macintosh ROM, but applications programs do not knock at the ROM door to talk to QuickDraw routines. Instead, QuickDraw facilities can only be reached indirectly. As a result, potentially nasty problems involving improperly written applications software programs are avoided.

QuickDraw defines some clear mathematical constructs that are widely used in its *procedures, functions,* and *data types:* the *coordinate plane,* the *point,* the *rectangle,* and the *region.*

All information about location, placement, or movement related to QuickDraw from a program, is supplied in terms of coordinates on a grid. The coordinate plane of QuickDraw has over 4.2 million unique points, with point (0,0) at the center of the grid. If two points are communicated to the QuickDraw package, it has all the information required to build a rectangle.

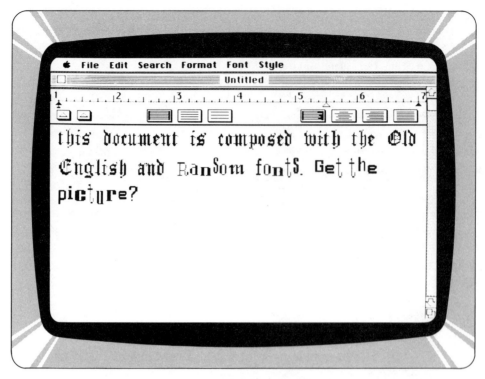

Fig. 5-3 Take your pick! You have the option of writing documents with terribly stuffy, formal fonts or outrageous typestyles.

The two points are construed to be the upper left and lower right corners of the rectangle.

Rectangles are frequently called to define active areas on the screen; to assign coordinate systems to graphic entities; and to specify the locations and sizes for various drawing commands. QuickDraw gives application software designers great flexibility in manipulating rectangles. Please bear in mind that none of this shows up directly on the Macintosh screen. These are purely mathematical operations, performed within the machine, that aren't tangible.

Dealing with rectangles efficiently is a delightful attribute but pretty limited. Just as in the real world, most figures can't be accurately described by a collection of rectangles. However, QuickDraw has the unique ability to gather a set of points that have some relationship to one another in two-dimensional space, and buzz through a lot of calculations to perform very complex, coherent manipulations of that relationship—even though the points are not related spatially in any way that resembles a regular geometric structure. In other words, the QuickDraw routines can work on the coordinates that describe the outline of an amoeba, and change the shape in a coherent

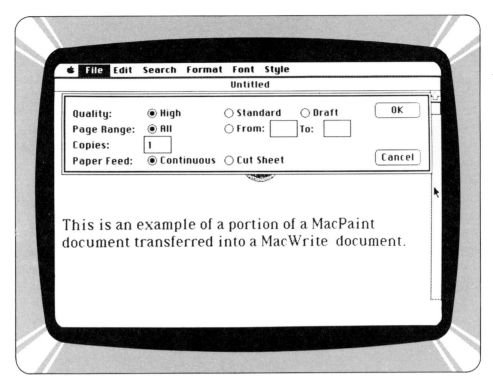

Fig. 5-4 Print parameters are easily set according to a checklist.

and predicted way. Without the QuickDraw routines to call into play, application programs could not bring into being or play with the weird shapes that can be described by Macintosh.

If a pattern is to be created on the screen, the QuickDraw routines treat it as a series of repeated dot cells (tiles of dimension 8 by 8). Within the cells are 64 independent dots of information (8 rows $\times$ 8 columns = 64 dots) that can have two states. You can picture each of the dots of information as containing a lightbulb. If the information represented in the dot has a high state, the lightbulb is on; if low, the light bulb is off. Viewed all at once, the individual dots of information within the cell form a figure. Many, many of the cells put edge to edge form a pattern.

To steer clear of the mountain of computation that would take until the next ice age, the smarts built into the QuickDraw routines split up the screen into arbitrary areas called *grafPorts*. Each grafPort is a complete drawing environment that defines how and where graphics operations will have their effect. It keeps all of the information about graphic events separate from other graphic events. The grafPorts are the structures with which an applications program builds windows. The grafPorts permit overlapping images without loss of coherence. Each grafPort has its own local coordinate system.

All calculations performed by QuickDraw use the local coordinate system of the grafPort being worked with at the time. Drawing always occurs in a grafPort.

The Resource Manager

So far, QuickDraw, the set of routines that creates all the graphics and text on Mac, has been discussed. The actual resources in ROM that set the Macintosh character—those that form menus, fonts, and icons—are generated by specific managers.

The specific managers for these system resources use a single resource manager. Below the single resource manager are specific device drivers which deal with the peculiarities of the hardware. This pyramid structure makes Mac both simple and powerful. By hiding the complexity at the lowest level and only presenting logical devices, the higher level software only sees a rational environment, or put another way, an ideal (virtual machine) environment.

THE SIXTH CHAPTER

An Electric Palette · Just Part of the Picture Shows
The Act of Creation · Smoothing the Edges
Text Is on Tap, Too · Memos Can Become Memorable

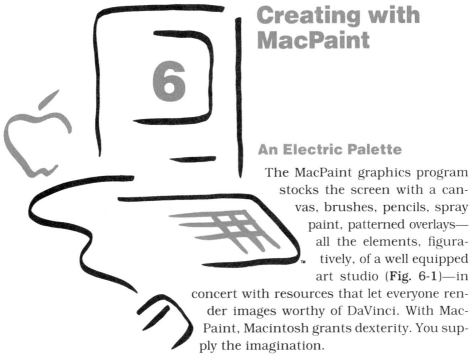

Creating with MacPaint

An Electric Palette

The MacPaint graphics program stocks the screen with a canvas, brushes, pencils, spray paint, patterned overlays—all the elements, figuratively, of a well equipped art studio (**Fig. 6-1**)—in concert with resources that let everyone render images worthy of DaVinci. With MacPaint, Macintosh grants dexterity. You supply the imagination.

When the MacPaint file icon or listing is opened from the Finder, a large paper (it looks like a canvas, too) spreads over the desktop. Along the left side of the desktop appear 20 symbols for utensils and operations. At the bottom of the desktop, a palette of 38 patterns becomes available for painting backgrounds, inserts, and lines.

A small box at the left lower corner of the desktop displays an inventory of lines in four widths that can be used to border figures.

Any of the items are at your disposal, as the artist, by use of the mouse. Positioning the pointer over an item and clicking the mouse button makes a selection.

The items at the bottom of the box on the left of the desktop represent types of *shapes* and *polygons* that can be drawn automatically, both *filled* and *unfilled.* Immediately above them, the item on the left, when selected, draws *rays* from a starting point to an end point selected by the pointer. Adjacent to that figure lies an indispensable tool for any artist; an *eraser*. It wipes clean areas of the canvas you drag it over (**Fig. 6-2A**). The two cells above show a *paint brush* and a *pencil,* respectively. The paint bucket symbol above the brush, when selected, fills an area of the canvas with whatever pattern is picked.

The *spray can* next to the paint bucket permits patterns to be *airbrushed* onto the document. In use, the spray can puts paint down in much the same way as its genuine model. In fact, a *brick wall* pattern can be *washed* over the document background by using the paint bucket icon. The spray can is used to apply a different pattern over the brick wall; electronic graffiti.

The "A" symbol above the spray can allows text to be typed into the art work. To the left of the "A" is a *hand icon.* When selected, the hand icon lets the pointer behave like a hand that has a grip on the artwork within the document. When the pointer is moved in that case, it moves all of the artwork as a unit within the window.

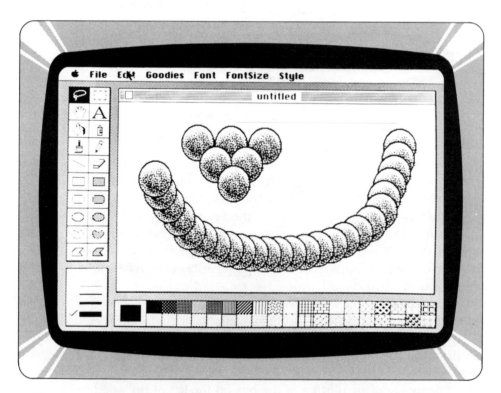

Fig. 6-1   Start with an empty canvas and render the beginnings of a masterpiece in five minutes with MacPaint.

Fig. 6-2A With the eraser icon, figures can be cleared like cleaning a blackboard.

Just Part of the Picture Shows

The window shows only about a third of the page space that is available within a MacPaint document, so artwork can be pushed aside beyond the area visible within the window. An entire document nearly fills an 8 1/2 by 11 inch page when printed.

To select an area within a drawing for changes, the *dotted rectangle* icon at the top of the list is selected. As the pointer is dragged across the screen, a blinking rectangle opens to envelop the area designated by the movement of the mouse. Whatever falls inside the rectangle is altered by any editing command (**Fig. 6-2B**). The area enclosed by the rectangle also can be dragged around the screen and relocated. As shown in **Figs. 6-3A** and **6-3B,** the lasso icon is used to select non-rectangular objects for the same operation.

The Act of Creation

Now that you have a better idea of your studio environment, we can explore what can be accomplished with the resources at your fingertips. For

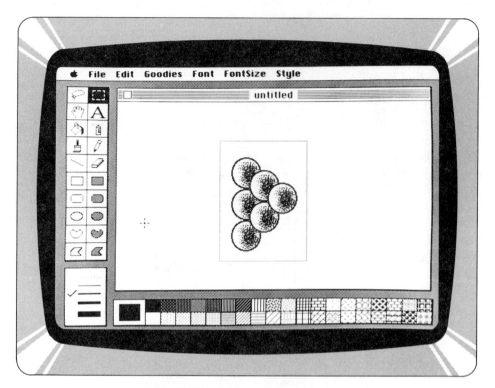

Fig. 6-2B **Editing in rectangle.**

starters, the displayed area of the MacPaint page can be washed with a background pattern selected from the palette at the bottom of the screen. This process simply requires putting the pointer over the desired pattern and clicking, then clicking the paint bucket icon in the column at the left side of the desktop. When the pointer is positioned anywhere over the paper and clicked, the pattern immediately fills the window.

The patterns on the palette themselves can be edited. A command designated *EDIT PATTERN* within the menu under the Goodies listing, shows a magnified view of the pattern at the pixel level and a corresponding view of the pattern as normally seen.

The paint brush icon paints broad strokes of the pattern you choose. The paint is applied in the pattern you describe by the motion of the mouse. You can be very, very exacting or you can set down free-form spashes as inspiration strikes.

If the width of the brush you're using doesn't meet your requirements, it can be changed by altering the brush shape. The process is like setting

Fig. 6-3A, 6-3B **Rope an area to be moved on the canvas and drag it to the new location!** ———————▶

A

B

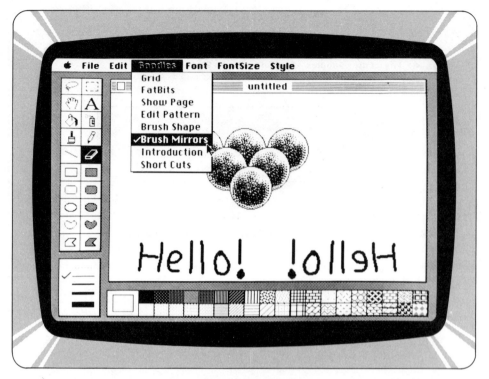

Fig. 6-4   Mirror images magically appear if the BRUSH MIRRORS
command is selected.

down a narrow sable brush and picking up a wide nylon one. A command
in the Goodies menu calls up a window with different *brush shapes* illustrated. There are over 30 possibilities. The brush shape in current use is
indicated by an outline.

To lay down symmetrical shapes, a special command, *BRUSH MIR-
RORS*, is available in the Goodies menu (**Fig. 6-4**). When that command is
invoked, a window appears superimposed on the document. There are quadrants in the window that can be selected that multiply the mirroring effect.

Smoothing the Edges

Please refer to the first **Fig. 6-1** in this chapter. Note the triangular group
of tennis balls. If you look at **Fig. 6-5**, you'll find that the tennis ball in the
upper left corner of the group is isolated in a small window within the document. The remainder of the window shows an area of the artwork magnified, so that each pixel within the inset is represented. By using the pencil
icon, the screen artwork can be refined at the pixel level. Pixels are the dots
on the screen that form images. To get this detailed view of a drawing, the
FATBITS command is selected. With this technique, remarkably detailed

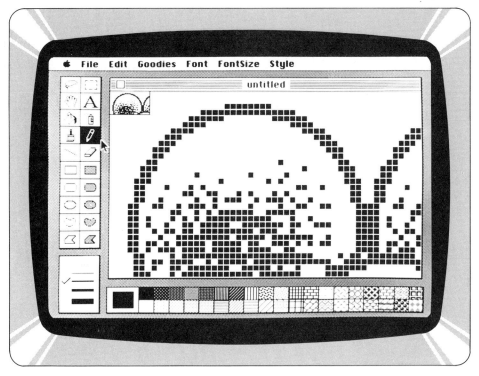

Fig. 6-5 Patterns can be tastefully edited by calling up a microscopic
view for pixel-by-pixel manipulation.

and elaborate drawings are possible. Minute variations in shading that lend
a three-dimensional perspective to figures can be arranged. Once the small
part of a work is refined, you can return to a full view of the document.

Copies of a figure can be made by using the rectangle or lasso to select
the figure to be duplicated, and pressing the OPTION key on the keyboard
while dragging the selected figure across the screen. This technique was
used to create the artwork in **Fig. 6-1**. To constrain the production of copies
to vertical or horizontal directions only, the SHIFT and command keys are
held down while the mouse is dragged. If the command key is depressed,
the figure can be stretched or shrunk by dragging the mouse in the direction
of expansion/contraction and then releasing the button.

The *rectangle* and *lasso* can be employed to select material that is to be
copied and pasted into another document. You can even remove part of a
MacPaint graphic document and add it to text created by the MacWrite word
processing program (**Fig. 6-6**). In the Edit menu, the *CUT*, *COPY*, and *PASTE*
commands can be applied for this purpose. The ability to transfer information from one program to a separate, unrelated program marks Mac as
an unusual machine indeed.

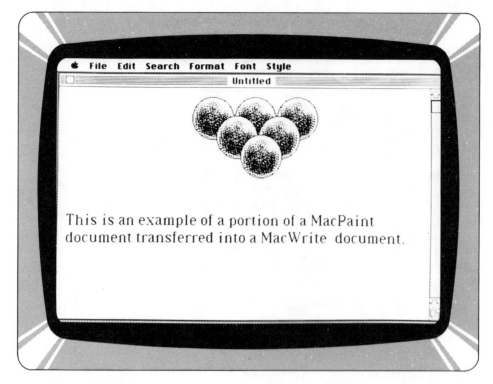

Fig. 6-6 **Artwork can be moved to the MacWrite environment.**

Images can be retained for long-term reapplication by sending them to the *scrapbook* for storage (**Fig. 6-7**). Images within the scrapbook are scrolled one at a time for review or transferred to the *Clipboard* for pasting in a document.

On the Edit menu, additional commands are available that quickly change the orientation of a selected area of the screen. You may flip horizontally or vertically, or rotate the area. This feature is particularly helpful when you need to prepare maps or other drawings which contain text which is non-horizontal. By first being drawn normally (left to right) and then rotated, we can achieve text which runs from bottom to top.

If you command Mac to perform an action which you would like to undo, your last editing action can be undone by applying the *UNDO* command from the Edit menu to bring back information as it appeared immediately before alteration. If you choose to return to the last version saved of a MacWrite document, pick the *REVERT* command from the File menu.

Text Is on Tap, Too

When the "A" box is selected, text can be applied to any area in a MacPaint document. A blinking vertical bar (I beam) marks the spot where

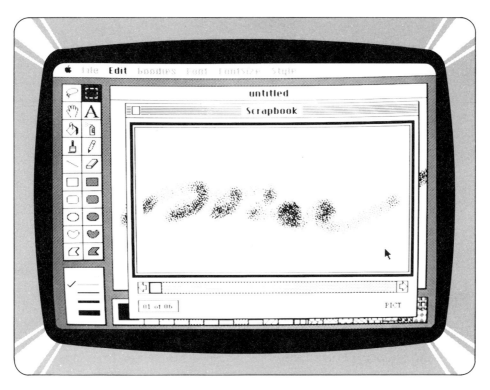

Fig. 6-7 Save figures in the scrapbook that are
to be duplicated frequently.

text is to be inserted. The text can be set down in any mixture of eight different *fonts* that can each be embellished by six different *style* decisions. Type can range in size from 9 to 72 *points*. The font, size, and style choices can be recast until the mouse button is clicked.

The labeling of figures is one obvious use for text in MacPaint artwork. Callouts can be *underlined* and *boldfaced* for particular emphasis. As a result, you can build diagrams for science reports or engineering documents. Schematics are easy to describe with the MacPaint program too. And just for fun, you can create mirror images by selecting the mirror function.

Should you wish to confine brush strokes or pencil lines to rectilinear description, the *GRID* command from the Goodies menu can be picked. This feature makes life particularly easy when you build diagrams.

The description of *hollow* and *filled rectangles*, *ellipses*, *amorphous figures*, and *irregular polygons* is facilitated by selections on the left side of the MacPaint desktop. Below the symbols that represent those figure choices, you can pick the width of a line used to border such figures. No coordinates are ever required to place a figure on a MacPaint document.

Memos Can Become Memorable

At the Apple Computer offices, memos have taken on a new dimension. Interoffice and intraoffice correspondence is prepared in great part on Macs. There is nothing humdrum about Apple memos; they buzz with pictures, boldface type that jumps out to put a date indelibly in mind, and pointers that set forth notable data. Since retyping is eliminated, the process of producing a memo with the Mac and an Imagewriter takes just a few minutes instead of hours.

Other applications within offices abound. For architects, Macintosh can spell a revolution. **Fig. 6-8** is an example of the complex detail that can be wrought on the Mac to describe a building. Hours of labor can be saved in the making of preliminary sketches for project review. A running shoe company can point out the salient details of new designs for sales training (see **Fig. 6-9**).

Interestingly, the first item in the Apple menu for MacPaint tells you that the program was created by Bill Atkinson in 1983. In fact, there's even a flattering picture of Bill included.

We've covered a lot of operations that can be performed with the Mac-Paint program. In reality, you can jump right into MacPaint without so much as a glance at any documentation. Nonetheless, there are two windows that give you a synopsis of MacPaint operations, which you can open from the

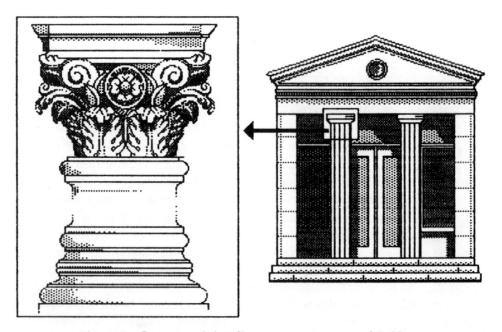

Fig. 6-8 Structural details are easy to map with Mac.

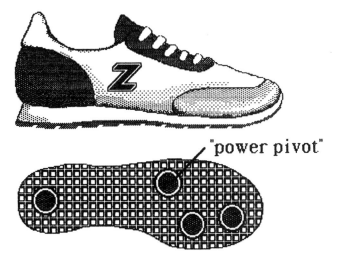

Fig. 6-9 Design updates can be issued quickly.

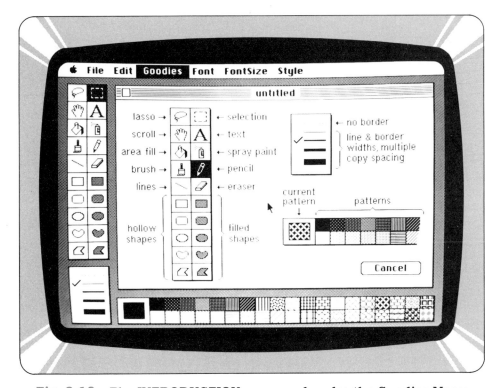

Fig. 6-10 The INTRODUCTION command under the Goodies Menu
presents a description of the MacPaint operations.

Goodies menu. INTRODUCTION, when selected (**Fig. 6-10**), presents a primer that describes the operations available within the MacPaint program.

SHORT CUTS lists painting operations and shortcuts to performing these same operations (**Fig. 6-11**), such as double clicking the mouse button, for certain menu selections.

To appreciate how great MacPaint is—what fun it can be and the rewards in productivity it affords—you have to try it first hand. So, grab your beret, leave the turpentine at home, and try it!

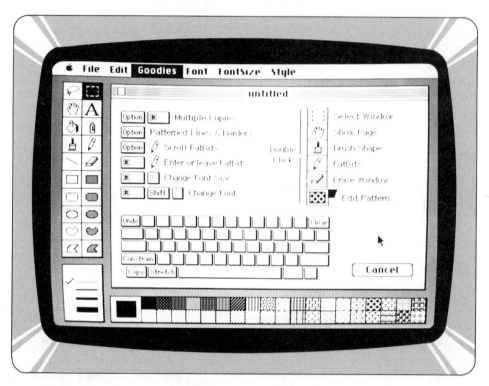

Fig. 6-11 The **SHORT CUTS** command under the Goodies Menu presents shortcut methods for performing MacPaint operations.

THE SEVENTH CHAPTER

You'll Like What You See • What's in It for You

Specials on the Menu • Fonts Can Be Fun

How to Find Fault • Edit with Ease

Paste in a Picasso

MacWrite a Novel Program

You'll Like What You See

MacWrite is a word processor package supplied by Apple with your Mac. The most remarkable thing about this package is that it is so easy to use. Rather than learning a jumble of codes to mark text and move things around, you simply point to what you want, and move it with a single key.

With some word processors, what you see on the screen is not what is printed on the paper. This leads to the need to prepare multiple printed versions till the final document agrees with what is on the screen. With MacWrite, "What you see is what you get."

What truly makes this word processing package superior to most others is its ability to mix pictures prepared in MacPaint with the text you prepare in MacWrite (this package). The result is a letter or memo with not only what you want to say, but with a picture too!

The MacWrite program is fast, delightfully easy to use and, above all, simple to understand. It can quickly streamline the flow of text and put the appearance of copy in fine order.

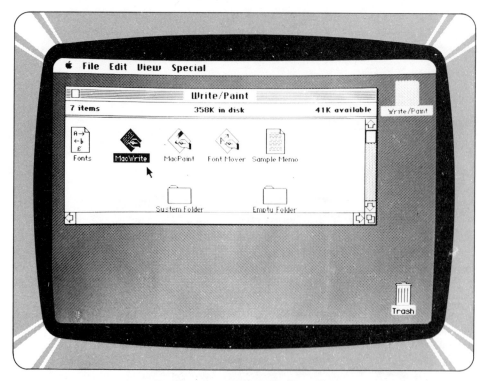

Fig. 7-1A Opening the MacWrite file listed on the Finder is the
first step to creating your epic.

What's in It for You

A MacWrite document can include paragraphs, pictures, or text from
other applications or desk accessories, and rulers that set text format. New
documents are automatically prepared according to a preset format that can
be rearranged at your discretion. The preset format defines page breaks at
8 1/2 inches, 1 inch top and bottom margins, and 1-1/8 inch left and right
margins.

The MacWrite program incorporates six types of windows: *Document*,
Header, *Footer*, *Clipboard*, *Find*, and *Change*. In most cases, a window is
opened by a command in a menu and closed, when active, by the close
command in the File menu or by clicking its Close box if it has one.

The *Document window* has a *scroll bar*. The Header, Footer, Clipboard,
and Document windows, all have *size boxes* that permits them to be expanded
or contracted when dragged by the cursor. Windows can be moved on the
desktop without being made active if they are dragged while the command
key is held down.

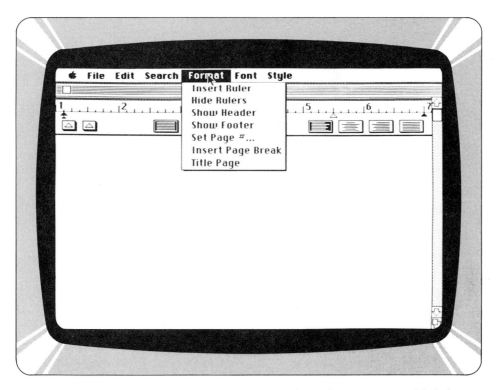

Fig. 7-1B Setting up the format of text in a document couldn't be easier: the format menu lets you do this step-by-step.

Specials on the Menu

Besides the standard menus in the program menu bar, MacWrite lists four menu headings: *Search, Format, Font,* and *Style*. Commands in the Format menu set the document mechanical specifications (**Fig. 7-1B**).

When a new document file is opened, a window appears with a ruler at the top and several symbols (**Fig. 7-2**). The ruler can be used to set *margins, paragraph indentation, regular* and *decimal tabs, line spacing,* and *text alignment*. Additional rulers can be inserted into text at any point when the *INSERT RULER* command is selected (**Fig 7-3A and 7-3B**).

The format set on one ruler sets the arrangement of text down to the next ruler. Margins are set by dragging arrow-shaped markers to the appropriate stops desired. To the left of each ruler, a small pointer with a bar at its base sets the paragraph indentations. The technique for setting paragraph indentations is the same as the one for setting margins.

You can set up to ten tabs on each ruler. There are two types of tabs: regular tabs, which align all text to the left, and decimal tabs, which align text to the right or at decimal points. Pressing the *TAB* key on the keyboard moves the insertion point for new text forward to the next tab position. If

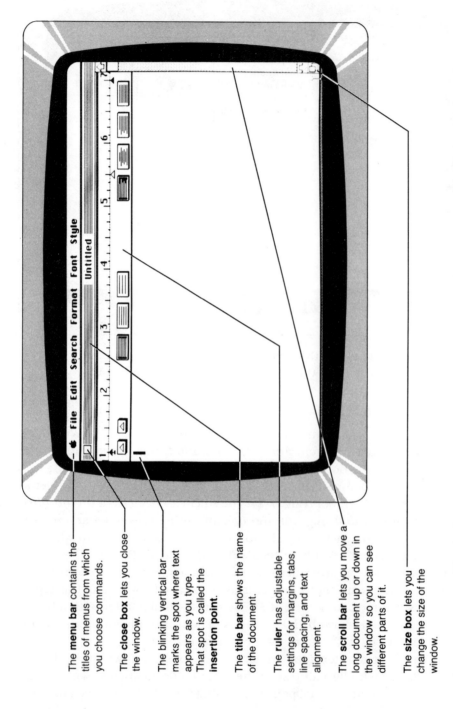

The **menu bar** contains the titles of menus from which you choose commands.

The **close box** lets you close the window.

The blinking vertical bar marks the spot where text appears as you type. That spot is called the **insertion point**.

The **title bar** shows the name of the document.

The **ruler** has adjustable settings for margins, tabs, line spacing, and text alignment.

The **scroll bar** lets you move a long document up or down in the window so you can see different parts of it.

The **size box** lets you change the size of the window.

Fig. 7-2 Rulers incorporate all the devices necessary to set up copy the way you want within the adjustable MacWrite windows.

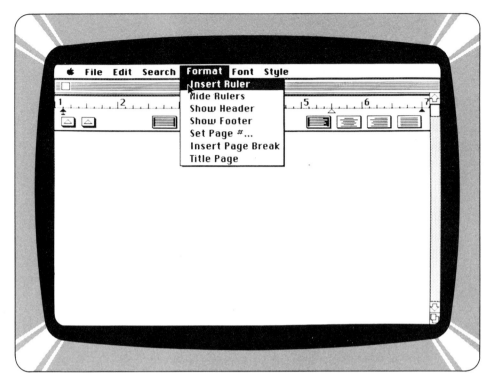

Fig. 7-3A Select the insert ruler command to alter the format of text when you're in the middle of a document.

there are no tab markers to the right of the insertion point, pressing the TAB key moves the insertion point forward to the first tab marker on the next line.

Tabs function as invisible characters that fill the space between the text and the marker position. As such, they can be edited as ordinary characters. To remove a tab, the space it occupies is selected and then cut by applying the *CUT* command in the Edit menu. Alternatively, tabs can be removed by backspacing.

Line spacing on a document can be set by clicking a cursor over one of three boxes along a ruler. You have the option of single-space, 1-1/2 space, and double-space increments.

The four boxes at the right of the rulers set *text alignment*. Text can be *left justified*, *centered*, *right justified*, or *justified* along both margins. Full justification does not alter the alignment of text at tabs.

The *HIDE RULERS* command on the Format menu makes all of the rulers within the text disappear. When the HIDE RULERS command is selected, the menu toggles to read *SHOW RULERS*.

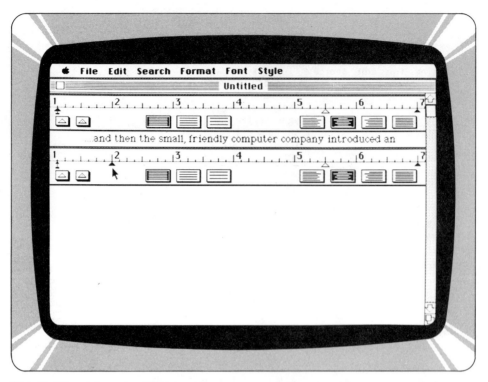

Fig. 7-3B After the INSERT RULER command is selected, another ruler pops into view to reformat text.

The *SHOW HEADER* command, which toggles to *HIDE HEADER* after being selected, opens the *Header window*. The *SHOW FOOTER* and *HIDE FOOTER* commands work the same way. The *header* and *footer* define top and bottom margins for every page of a document. In addition to blank lines, a header or footer can contain lines of text, pictures, page numbers, the time from the desk accessory clock and the date. Each document can contain one header, one footer, or both.

The header and footer are created separately in their respective header and footer window. When the document window is active, they are displayed on each page of the document. Hiding or closing the header or footer window removes the header or footer from view in the document window and in printed copy.

The header window presents a ruler along with three symbols for locating the *time*, *page number*, and *date* in the same manner that parameters are set on the ordinary MacWrite ruler (**Fig. 7-4A**). The footer window presents the three symbols too (**Fig. 7-4B**).

The command for setting the page number, when selected, puts the number of the first page in the document unless the *TITLE PAGE* command

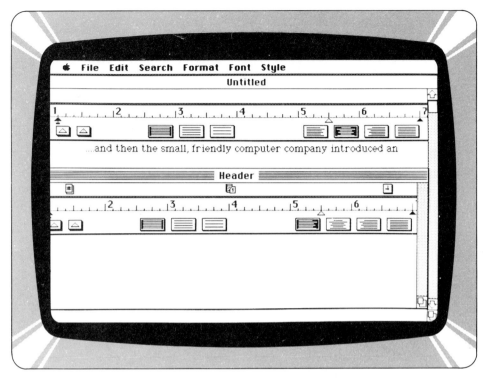

Fig. 7-4A **Headers apply qualifying information to MacWrite document pages.**

is selected. The *TITLE PAGE* command causes the header or footer not to appear on the first page of the document.

The *INSERT PAGE BREAK* command forces a page break by inserting blank space to take up the remainder of an open page. If text is added or removed subsequently ahead of the page break, the space is resized to accommodate the changes.

Fonts Can Be Fun

The *Font menu* (**Fig. 7-5**) displays a choice of nine different fabulous fonts that can be switched at any point within the text. These fonts can be mixed in any way you please. The *Style menu* commands (**Fig. 7-6**) work in conjunction with a selected font. There are nine different type sizes that can be chosen from the Style menu, which range from 9 to 72 points. In addition to unembellished text, commands can create *boldfaced entries*, *italic characters*, *underlined text*, *outlined characters*, and *shadowed copy*. Horizontal and vertical line spacing is automatically adjusted to accommodate the largest character in a line.

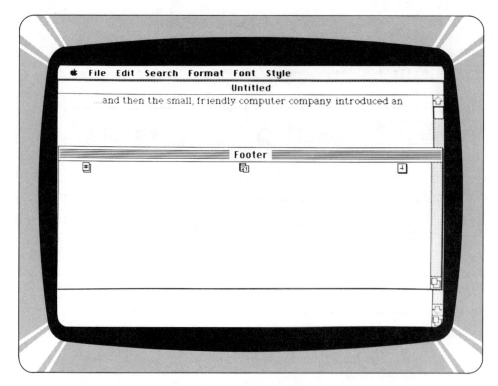

Fig. 7-4B   Footers put information beneath texts.

How to Find Fault

The Search menu has two commands, *FIND* and *CHANGE* (**Fig. 7-7**). The *FIND* command finds and selects, in the active window, the next occurrence of your search text. It opens the *Find window*, in which the text to be found is specified. You can use up to 44 characters of text to be found. Text can be moved or copied between the Document window and the Find window. The text within the Find window itself can be selected and edited.

Inside the Find window is a button labeled *FIND NEXT*; clicking it begins the search. The search starts at the selection, proceeds to the end of the document, wraps back to the beginning, and ends where it began. If the specified text is found in the document, the occurrence is selected. The found text can be edited, once the document is activated.

The *FIND* command searches for an exact character-for-character match and ignores capitalization, accents on characters, fonts, sizes, and styles. If the text you are searching for isn't found, a message will inform you. The close box in the Find window's *Title bar* or the *CLOSE* command in the File menu closes an active Find window.

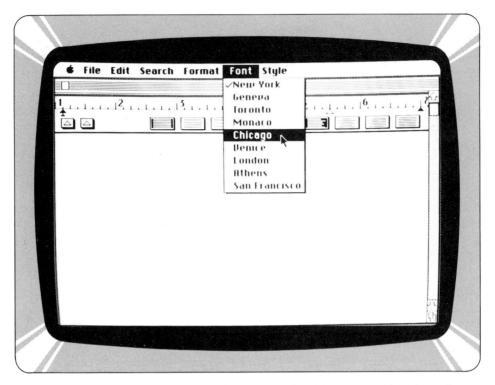

Fig. 7-5 There are fonts in this menu suited for everything from love
letters to ransom notes.

The *CHANGE command* in the Search menu not only permits you to
search for a specific text in the most recently active window, but it also allows
the found text to be automatically changed according to an entry in the
Change window. The two rectangles within the window, *FIND WHAT* and
CHANGE TO, can each hold 44 characters of text. Clicking the *CHANGE
THEN FIND* button replaces the current selection with the contents of the
CHANGE TO rectangle.

Edit with Ease

Commands in the Edit menu of MacWrite include *UNDO, CUT, COPY,
PASTE*, and *SHOW CLIPBOARD*. There are equivalent keyboard commands
listed in the menu for those operations.

The *CUT* command removes selected text, rulers, pictures, and page
breaks (**Fig. 7-8**). Anything cut from a document winds up in the Clipboard
(**Fig. 7-9**). Material previously stored in the Clipboard is replaced by the new
material.

When the *COPY* command is chosen, selected material from a document
is duplicated in the Clipboard but is not deleted from a document. The

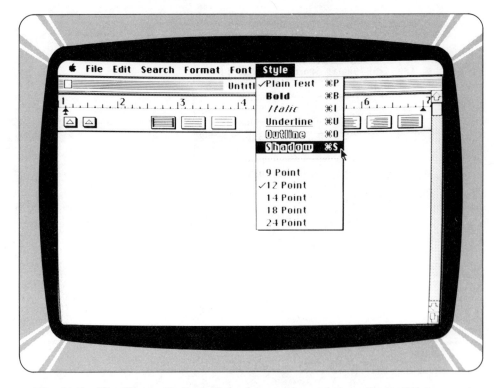

Fig. 7-6 Headlines that can't be ignored can be applied with 24 point type. If you get bored with the stock fonts, add highlights from the Style menu.

PASTE command replaces a selection within a document with the contents of the Clipboard. Once accomplished, the insertion point moves to the end of the pasted-in material. Rulers, page breaks, and pictures cannot be pasted into the Find or Change windows, nor into most desk accessories.

Paste in a Picasso

Artwork generated in the MacPaint graphics program can be transplanted to MacWrite documents in the same manner that text is cut, copied, moved, and pasted. The contents of the Clipboard are retained independently of the program environment they came from on the disk.

A picture moved to a MacWrite document can be resized and shifted horizontally. The picture is scaled in proportion as it is resized within the document. When the cursor is placed anywhere on the picture and the mouse button is clicked, a black dotted rectangular outline appears around the figure. Three small black boxes dot the bottom of the rectangle; one at the left, one at the right, and one in the middle.

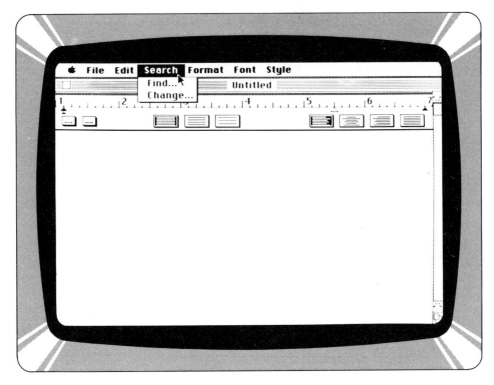

Fig. 7-7 To locate information within text, choose the FIND command. To not only locate but also change information, select the CHANGE command.

Dragging the cursor on any of the boxes resizes the picture. The middle box moves the bottom border vertically to lengthen or shorten the picture. The left and right boxes move the bottom and the corresponding edge to change the width and/or length of the picture. To move the figure horizontally, the cursor is dragged on the right or left side of the rectangle that surrounds the picture. In this manner, detailed illustrated texts can be composed entirely on screen, then sent to the Imagewriter for final copy.

When you complete a MacWrite document and elect to CLOSE the file, Mac double checks to make sure that you store the information you want. You also get the option of returning to the document and not closing the file (**Fig. 7-10**).

Given the facilities within the MacWrite program—different fonts, type styles, format aids, and editing resources—along with the ability to transfer art from the MacPaint program, you can produce complete manuals. Or, you can write a film treatment that includes sketches of how you visualize a scene. You might like to create illustrated bedtime stories especially for your children. MacWrite lights your imagination.

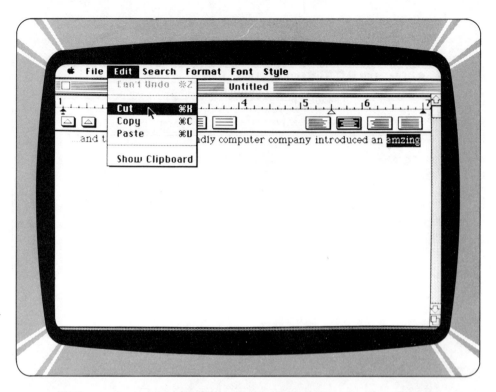

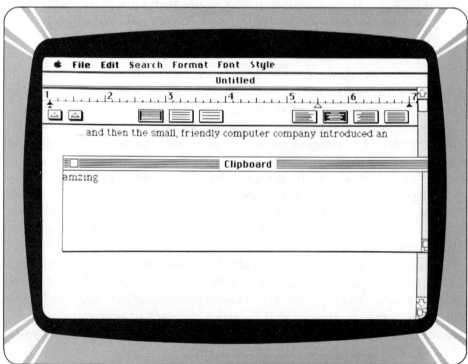

Fig. 7-8 Forget the scissors! Macintosh removes
information from a document when the CUT command is called to
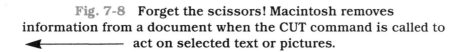 act on selected text or pictures.

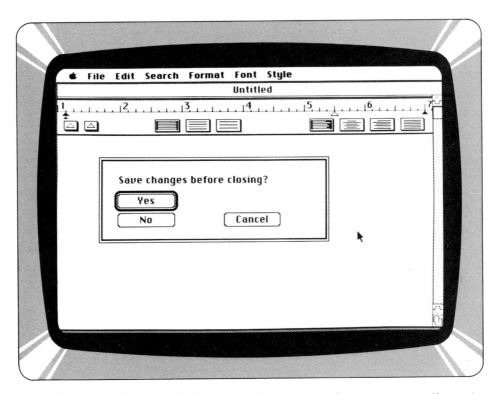

Fig. 7-10 At the completion of work, you can elect to save or discard
entries, or return to the document.

Fig. 7-9 Whatever is snipped from documents winds
up in the Clipboard. As new information is CUT, it displaces
the previous entry in the Clipboard.

THE EIGHTH CHAPTER

Coming Soon . . .

Mac Fits into an Office System

There's Still More from Apple

Coming Soon . . .

Now that you're up to speed on MacWrite and MacPaint, two programs available right off the bat from Apple for Mac, let me tell you about some terrific Apple programs that will be coming.

Coming soon to an Apple dealer near you is the *MacTerminal* program. With the MacTerminal program and an Apple Modem, you will be able to put your Macintosh on-line with the vast world of data bases.

This software package allows you to connect to the latest stock market quotations, stay on top of international political developments, or track your horoscope every day. An enormous amount of information and services will be at your fingertips. You can tap into electronic bulletin board services that connect you with grass roots happenings among other computer enthusiasts.

The MacTerminal program will allow Mac to emulate the VT-l00 and VT-52 terminals manufactured by Digital Equipment Corporation. With this program, Macintosh will even be able to function in an IBM environment by being able to emulate the IBM 3270 workstation.

Also for release from Apple is Macintosh *Pascal*, with all of the resources you'll need to learn how to create programs for your Mac. In addition to Pascal, the software you need for *BASIC* programming will also be available.

If you liked building Logo programs on the Apple II, you'll love Macintosh *Logo*, which will also be available.

Programs that were once only available on the Lisa will be brought over to the Mac.

* MacProject—Project management program
* MacDraw—Object oriented graphics package similar to MacPaint
* Assembler/Debugger—Software tools for machine language work

Concurrent with the introduction of Macintosh, Apple has introduced the *Lisa 2*. The Lisa 2 consists of many different versions of Lisa which are new, upgraded versions of the original Lisa. They can incorporate a 5 or 10 megabyte integral hard-disk drive, 512 Kbytes or 1 megabyte, and also have microfloppy disk drives that accept Macintosh software. Lisa 2 is the principal development environment for Mac application software.

Mac Fits into an Office System

The constraints of this book limit our focus to Macintosh almost exclusively, but you should be aware that Mac is not an isolated personal productivity tool, but part of an integrated family of Apple products with advanced 32-bit architecture.

To link all of the different machines in the Apple family, Apple has developed what is known as the *Applebus*. The Applebus physically links productivity resources to build super streamlined office information systems. The Applebus is designed to support the 32-bit family of machines as well as the Apple II.

The Applebus communications scheme links up to 32 workstations and shared resources on a twisted pair of lines of up to 1,000 feet from end to end. The link, which is based mechanically on RS-422, can pass 230.4 Kbits of information per second between productivity stations.

A typical implementation of the 32-bit family interfaces distributed stations and a PABX system within an office. Shared resources can include a laser printer, 20 megabyte file server, an in-office data base on a 70 megabyte hard-disk, and gateway to remote networks in other communications environments. As planned, the communications gateway will permit the Apple 32-bit system to hook up with other office networks that are based on Ethernet, SNA, X.25, and the forthcoming IBM LAN schemes.

Ethernet, SNA, X.25, and the new network architecture being booked up at IBM are elaborate hardware and software standards to facilitate intercommunications among a group of workstations and office resources. These local-area network schemes have about as much in common as Japanese and Peruvian cultures. The fact that the Apple communications server can provide access to all these markedly different and exclusive networks, and more, brings extraordinary flexibility to the Apple 32-bit family of office productivity resources.

We will see Macs hooked into many, many Apple 32-bit system environments. The Macintosh machine covers a lot of territory.

The Third Slice:

The MacVironment

THE NINTH CHAPTER

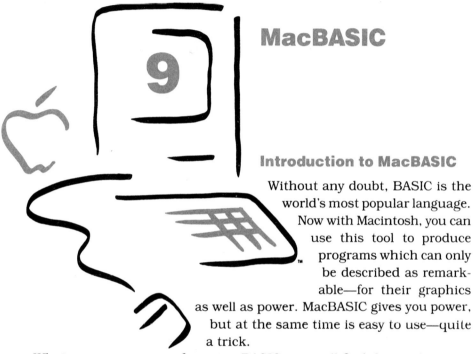

MacBASIC

Introduction to MacBASIC

Without any doubt, BASIC is the world's most popular language. Now with Macintosh, you can use this tool to produce programs which can only be described as remarkable—for their graphics as well as power. MacBASIC gives you power, but at the same time is easy to use—quite a trick.

Whatever your reasons for using BASIC, you will find the implementation of MacBASIC probably the most powerful. Where does this power stem from you may ask? New peripherals, a powerful microprocessor, and superior software account for its incredible performance.

This new version of BASIC for the Mac incorporates the mouse (that thing you roll around) in all aspects of its operation. Consider for a moment the situation of having to change a program. You have to search through a listing for the proper line and then give a normal BASIC a series of cursor control instructions to get to the point of change. With the mouse, you simply point to where you want make the change and click the button on the mouse.

The use of a mouse in connection with multiple windows makes the job of working with BASIC programs much easier to deal with. MacBASIC incorporates separate windows for *commands*, *listings* and *screen output*. Using the ease of movement that a mouse gives, plus the ability to move windows as well as scroll them, makes MacBASIC a dream come true.

While all of this may seem quite irrelevant to you, you too can make use of these powerful window features. In fact, what we have not told you yet is that you have access to the screen to do all sorts of graphics. If you are interested in report generation, or are interested in producing graphs for scientific experiments, you can use the Mac as your partner—the one who can produce fabulous drawings which always get a great response.

For those who have used other BASICs, you will find the MacEngine (68000 microprocessor) brings with it the answer to all of the nagging problems which have driven you to put an ax through your machine.

The use of a *68000 microprocessor* (MacEngine) in Mac brings with it two aspects which make MacBASIC fundamentally different from other implementations of BASIC in personal computers. The first aspect is the ability of the microprocessor in Mac to address up to 16 million characters of information. While the internal memory of the Mac is not that large, it does take full advantage of its available memory. Probably the most important aspect of Mac's microprocessor is its ability to deal with numbers more efficiently than early generations of microprocessors. This aspect translates into faster results when BASIC is working, as well as more robust graphics.

You may be a little intimidated by this point and feeling, "all of this power is great but I don't want to learn another version of BASIC—it was hard enough learning the first one!" Take heart, this BASIC is really substantially the same as that which is found on most personal computers. Almost all of the *commands* and *keywords* work exactly as you would expect. What is different then? The primary differences between this BASIC and others produced by Microsoft relate to the characteristics of the peripherals hooked up to Mac. What this means then is that if you write programs which do not take advantage of Mac's display characteristic, this BASIC will seem quite unremarkable and as familiar as any BASIC. These enhancements to BASIC were intended to supplement the standard versions of BASIC—we call this *upward compatibility*. Upward compatibility refers to the ability of this BASIC to run BASIC programs written for earlier machines but with the use of more advanced features of MacBASIC being optional.

The designers at Microsoft (the designers of MacBASIC) took a quantum jump in software engineering when they produced MacBASIC. At the same time they remembered that for you to get the maximum benefit out of their new BASIC, they would have to make it as compatible as possible with your existing programs written in other variations of BASIC—true human engineering in this case means making your transition to Mac as pleasant as possible.

On the BASIC Menu We Have . . .

MacBASIC (properly referred to as Microsoft BASIC) is contained on a disk and needs to be started in the same manner as other Mac tools. We will go over that procedure next.

After turning on the Mac, you should insert the disk containing the MacBASIC tool. After about 20 seconds the *icons* will appear which represent the programs contained on the disk. At this point you should move the mouse to the icon marked MS-BASIC. Once you are on the icon, press the button on the mouse twice; this causes the MacBASIC tool to be loaded into Mac and started.

Once loaded, let's examine what's on the screen and how it relates to what we know about BASIC. Pictured in **Fig. 9-1** is the display after loading MacBASIC. At the top of the screen is the Title menu which is common to all Mac tools. In the menu we see four selections:

Apple Logo is used to allow access to Mac's desk accessories such as the calculator, control panel, date/time display and other assorted accessories (**Fig. 9-2**).

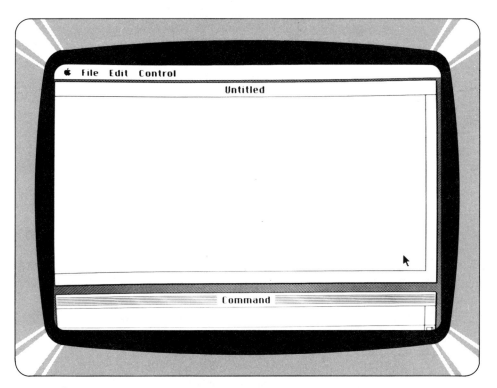

Fig. 9-1 After loading MS-BASIC, the screen looks like this.

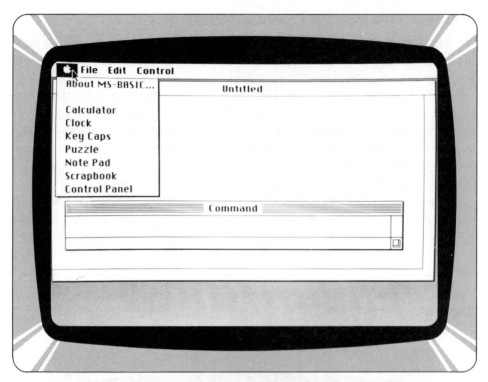

**Fig. 9-2   The Apple menu selection contains the standard
desk accessories.**

File (**Fig. 9-3**) supplies the escape hatch from MacBASIC when you want
to return to the Finder menu (master menu). It is also used to load from,
and store programs to the disk.

Edit (**Fig. 9-4**) options allows you to CUT, COPY, or PASTE in your program. The actual editing of lines can be accomplished by simply pointing
the mouse at the line to be modified and clicking (pressing) the button on
the mouse. This copies the line into the Command window—more on this
later.

Control (**Fig. 9-5**) allows you to select the common program control
instructions such as *RUN, STOP, CONTINUE, TRACEON, TRACEOFF* and
a command to suspend the program. These commands may be typed in of
course, but their placement on the menu is designed as an alternative method
of controlling BASIC.

The menu bar is designed to make life easier by allowing you to control
the operation of BASIC programs with the mouse. In some cases it may be
simpler to use the keyboard to just tell Mac what you want.

An example of how you can use either method would be to describe the
method of starting a program with the RUN instruction.

With the mouse, you would position the pointer (arrow) below the Control legend on the menu bar. Once positioned, you would then press and

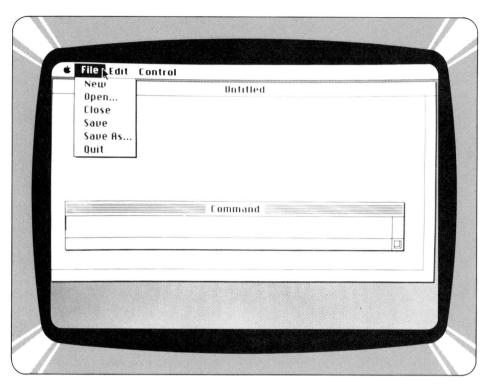

Fig. 9-3 The File menu is used to load from, and store
programs to disk.

hold the mouse button, at which time the list of selections would appear below the Control legend. You would then proceed to move the pointer to the selection marked RUN. You have visual feedback from the screen on your selection as the one selected will be in black while all others are in white. By releasing the button while the RUN selection is black, you can cause the RUN command to be received by BASIC.

While these instructions may seem complicated, they really are quite natural. What you are doing is reaching into a box and pulling out a menu of options and pointing to the one you want.

If we wanted to perform the RUN operation manually we would type in RUN and press the Enter key. Surprisingly, even though this sounds simpler, for persons who are not speed typists or computer gurus, the use of the mouse is preferable. Sometimes the obvious "right way" to do things isn't what you might expect.

BASIC Windows

We should digress at this point and discuss the structure of the multiple windows and what their purposes are. First off, there are really three windows which you will be dealing with; these are the *Command window*,

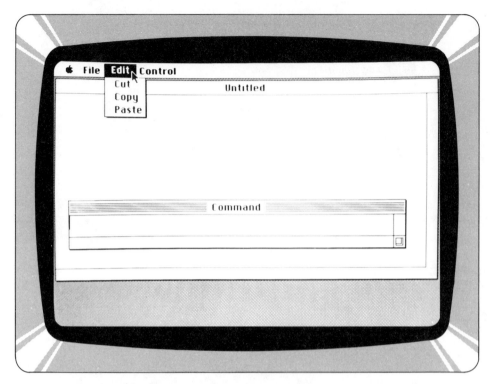

Fig. 9-4 **The Edit menu selections will let you CUT, COPY or PASTE in a program.**

Output window and *List window*. Each has a well defined function—all working in concert to create a flexible and friendly environment for programming as well as usage.

The Command Window

When you wish to talk to MacBASIC with the keyboard, you interact via what is called the *Command window* (**Fig. 9-6**). The Command window is used for the input and editing of programs as well as the direct control of BASIC. If you have experience with BASIC on other machines, you can look at the Command window as the current line you are typing.

With the line in the Command window, you can use the mouse to reposition the *type-in cursor* by moving the mouse to the desired position, then pressing the button on the mouse. Another capability is that of being able to remove groups of characters in the line with the mouse. This is accomplished by moving the pointer to the start of the character to be removed, then pressing and holding the button down. By moving the mouse with the button down across the line, you will see characters change to black. When you release the button, all of the characters which were turned black will

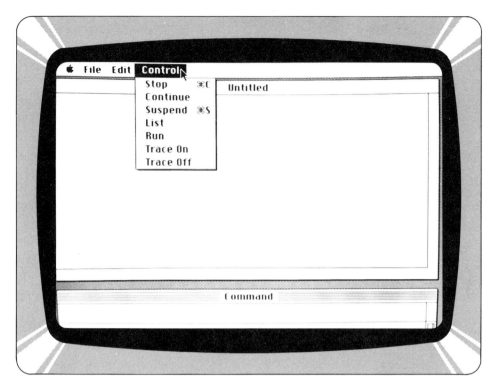

Fig. 9-5 **The Control menu contains common BASIC program control instructions.**

stay black. You can then remove these characters by selecting the CUT option on the Edit menu. This editing feature makes line editing more straightforward than in simple systems.

If we could only edit the current line we were typing, we would be quite limited. Fortunately Microsoft give us a way to edit *any line* in the program. We will look at how to do that in the next section.

Another feature of the Command window is its ability to change size. If you place the mouse pointer in the top bar of the window and press the mouse button, you can drag the window up the screen. By then releasing the button you can have it take on its new position. To open the size of the window, you would position the pointer in the lower right bottom square of the window. By pressing and holding the button you can now stretch the window downward by moving the mouse down. The final size of the window will be that at which you left it when you released the button of the mouse. You should be aware of this ability to change size since you may encounter lines in the Command window larger than the size of the window. Those lines which extend beyond the window are not lost but are simply not displayed. You can, of course, see these windows by extending the window size, as we have described.

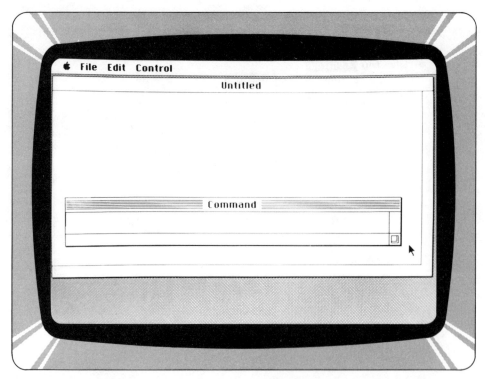

Fig. 9-6   **The Command window is used for input and editing of programs as well as direct control of BASIC.**

The List Window

In the process of preparing a program, we spend a great deal of time entering a program and listing it. In a typical system, we would use the same screen for input as for output. This is not a bad decision, but what would happen if we were interested in observing more than one area at a time? In the case of two areas, we would perform two listings. With Mac, we can open up two *List windows* and see these two groups of lines *simultaneously.* This ability to deal with multiple areas of our program makes Mac much more friendly when being used in program development work when compared with conventional systems.

The *List window* has a peculiar character though. When MacBASIC first starts up, there are only two windows shown: Output and Command. Where is the List window? The answer is: there is none yet. When first started, the MacBASIC only shows these two windows. To bring in a fresh List window, either type LIST and press ENTER; or select the LIST option on the Control menu with the mouse. A List window is created when the LIST command is executed.

Once a LIST command has been entered, the window created by the command is permanently on the screen. At this point we will have three (3) windows on the screen. The only thing is that there is really not enough room on the screen for so many windows, so some will become obscured. This means we have to have some way of specifying the *precedence* of windows, or in other words, which window goes in front of which other window.

The determination of window precedence is determined by two methods. The first way of selecting the order is by the use of the mouse and button to tell Mac we want to see a window up front (made visible by being moved on top). To move a window to the top, we move the mouse pointer to an area of that window which is visible and click the button; this will cause the window to be displayed top of all others.

Manual selection with the mouse is used to select the prioritization of all windows on the screen. If we first wanted to see the List window, we would select that one. If we then wanted to see another List window, we would find a piece of that window which was visible and then select it. If we wanted to see the Output window, we would then point to a portion of it and then press the mouse button, which would cause it to take precedence over the windows obscuring it.

In addition to being able to control the precedence of the windows, we can rearrange the positioning of the windows by positioning the pointer at the top of a window, and then pressing and holding the button to drag the box into another position.

Now that we know how to make a List window visible, we can perform a few more tricks with it. The most useful is the ability to scroll. When we perform a LIST and a window is created for the program, we can view not only the first few lines of the program, but the entire program too. But you say, "the window is so small, how can I view a large program?" The answer is that the List window only shows a small portion of what it is capable of showing.

When first created, the List window is quite small in size. We can enlarge it by first moving it up the screen by using the top of the List window to drag it into a new position. We would then expand it by using the box in the bottom right of the window to stretch it. But even so, we still will not be able to see the entire program. We can scroll through the program by means of scroll bars located on the right and bottom of the List window.

Each of the scroll bars is used to move the view. The scroll bar located vertically along the right side of the screen is used to scroll up and down through the program. This bar is used by moving the pointer to one of the arrows and pressing the key on the mouse. If the key is held down, the window will continuously scroll through the program till the key is released. If we want to go to a specific area in the program, we can position the pointer on the square box located between the arrows and drag it to the position we would like by pressing the button down and holding; then moving the mouse till it is located in the proper position.

If we would like to create a List window starting at a certain position, we can do that too by typing: LIST *linenumber*. This specific *linenumber* command will do exactly what it says: create a List window which is at *linenumber*.

Every time we create a new window with the LIST command, another new window is created and added to our current collection. All of the previous List windows are retained on the screen. You may be wondering how one would go about getting rid of all of these extra List windows? The answer lies in the fact that most windows used by Mac have a small square located in the top left corner of their windows. If you put the tip of the arrow of the pointer in this square and momentarily press the mouse button, the entire window will be removed—it's that simple to remove a window.

We can therefore see that the LIST feature of MacBASIC is quite a bit more powerful than anything currently available. Its ability to scroll, flip between windows, and change size allows us much more freedom to determine the optimum listing format.

The Output Window

We now have some idea as to how to see what the output looks like, and how to command Mac to start and control our program. The best part of programming is the interaction between you, the user, and the program. This interaction goes on in the *Output window*, which is the third and largest window. This window is used to echo your input lines when inputting your program as well as supplying output in both textual as well as graphical form.

To understand the Output window, we need to analyze the two situations in which it is used. The first case is when we are in Command mode—not running a program. In this case, the output window will be overlaid every time we ask for the List window or move the Command window over the Output window. To reestablish the top priority of the Output window, just place the mouse in the interior of the Output window and momentarily press the button on the mouse.

Whenever we start up a program by invoking the RUN command, the entire set of windows on the screen is changed. The Command window is removed from the screen (all input is via the Output window) and the List window is placed behind the Output window. This ordering is both logical and reduces clutter on the screen. If we want to look at the List window, we can point at its window and momentarily press the button. The effect of this action during a program run would be to terminate the currently running program and cause the List window to appear on top of the Output window.

Not to be outdone by the other windows, we can modify the size and placement of the Output window too. When MacBASIC is first started up, the size of the Output window is such that when the program stops, the Command window will appear just below it.

The Output window has a rich variety of commands in MacBASIC which make it easy to use. One of the pleasant surprises that also makes MacBASIC unique is that it supplies you with a predefined set of symbols which may be "called" to supplement the built-in BASIC functions. These extra symbols allow you access to the built-in Mac ROM functions which give Mac its graphics capabilities.

Beyond Standard BASIC

We mentioned earlier in this chapter that MacBASIC was upward compatible with standard Microsoft BASIC. We will now examine what features extend and enhance the capabilities of standard BASIC.

First off, since we have a high resolution bit-mapped screen, we have commands to draw lines and circles. Since such a large amount of information is stored on the screen, we have a set of commands, called GET and PUT, which transfer points on the screen to arrays in BASIC. This feature improves the transfer efficiency of graphics transfers to secondary storage, such as a disk.

At the beginning of the chapter we also mentioned that there are extra peripheral capabilities in the Mac which MacBASIC could tap through its language extensions. The device we were referring to is the mouse. Through MacBASIC we can interrogate the position of the mouse as well the position of the push button. Conditions reported from the mouse include:

- Button up
- Button down
- Single-click
- Double-click
- Drag

The more powerful processor available in the Mac gives us greater ability to manipulate numbers at high speed. Unlike earlier versions of BASIC, MacBASIC assumes all variables are double precision. Most of the functions in MacBASIC also return double precision values. Double precision variables are stored with 17 character precision and printed with up to 16 digits.

For business applications, the MacBASIC *Decimal Math Package* provides 14-digit precision in math operations. This high degree of precision is absolutely necessary when performing business calculations, since there is no round-off error.

This extra data processing capability even extends to Mac's capabilities with strings. In most implementations of BASIC, strings are limited in length to 255 characters. In Mac, strings can extend in length to 32,767 characters. For users who just needed "one more character" to complete their string handling package, this is truly an answer to their prayers.

Another area in which early BASIC versions were lacking was in array size. Most early versions were very limited in the number of dimensions as well as the size of the index. In MacBASIC, you can have up to 255 dimensions. The maximum number of elements per dimension is 32,768. This means that you can store very large arrays that would not even be conceivable in earlier machines.

Usually only found on larger machines, the Mac incorporates *Device Independent I/O* which makes all devices in the system appear to be the same. This means writing to the printer is an identical procedure to opening a disk file. This device independence also includes writing to devices which are not even what would be considered real—an example would be the Clipboard.

MacBASIC Summary

After reviewing all of the capabilities in the MacBASIC package, you can conclude that the combination of the Mac's microprocessor, Microsoft MacBASIC and the capabilities of the Mac, make MacBASIC the best BASIC there is.

THE TENTH CHAPTER

The Power of Multiplan

Starting up MacMultiplan • What's in a Plan

If You Can't Put It in Numbers, It's Not Real

A Formula for Everything • Special Effects I—Multiple Windows

Special Effects II—Frozen Titles • Even More

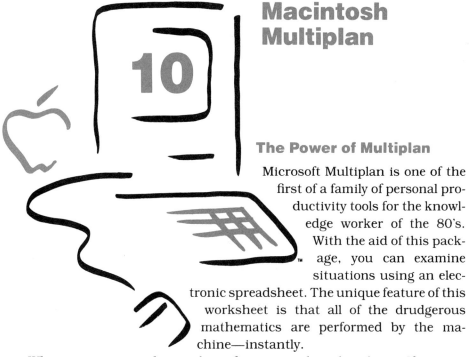

Macintosh Multiplan

The Power of Multiplan

Microsoft Multiplan is one of the first of a family of personal productivity tools for the knowledge worker of the 80's. With the aid of this package, you can examine situations using an electronic spreadsheet. The unique feature of this worksheet is that all of the drudgerous mathematics are performed by the machine—instantly.

What can you use this package for you might ask—plenty. If you are currently doing capital budgeting, making major sales force decisions, analyzing product planning, or are responsible for cash flow planning, you'll get hooked faster than you'll believe. If you are interested in scientific pursuits such as engineering, construction, or even physics, you'll find that Multiplan's ability to organize and easily digest information will make life much easier.

The power of Multiplan is in its ability to both hold and process information. Coupling the information with formulas which you can easily understand and change, you can perform what are known as "what-if" strategies. An example of this might be the case of a company which is trying to determine the best mix of products to sell. Working within the constraints of available capital, manpower, and space, we can create a model of the company and juggle the figures to optimize the use of resources for maximum return. This strategy was only available to the largest of companies 5 years ago, but today, with Mac and Multiplan, you are on an equal footing.

But how does Multiplan work—and is this some sort of foreign program full of strange symbols and concepts or can someone like me really understand it—and most important, can I use it for something useful? It's not hard to understand; and yes, there are a tremendous number of things you can do with it.

If you can, imagine a large sheet of ledger paper (the kind an accountant uses) in which you can write in figures. The screen of the computer is laid out just like a spreadsheet (**Fig. 10-1**). To enter a figure somewhere on the sheet, point to where you want to make the entry, click the mouse, and enter the number.

If you could only write numbers on the sheet and recall them, this alone would make the computer useful—but then all it would be is a filing cabinet. There is more. The true power of Multiplan is that you can have these figures digested automatically. In effect, you put the figures you have into little boxes on the screen, and in others you put in formulas that describe what you want to do with the figures. What happens next is absolutely fas-

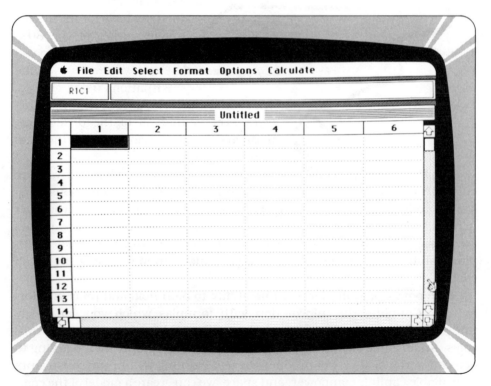

Fig. 10-1 **The Multiplan Screen looks like a spreadsheet.**

cinating—in just a fraction of a second, all of your numbers are digested and the results appear.

You perform what-if analysis as a two part process. One way to do analysis is to vary the numbers and see how they affect the results. The second method is to modify the formulas and see what effect they have on the results.

In the case of modifying the numbers, this would be the case when you have limited resources and you would like to see the effects of redistribution. One of the best examples of this application would be the distribution of different salesmen in a territory. You might determine that a salesman is not justified based on the sales volume generated. On the other hand you may find that you could put even more salespersons in a territory. In the case of additional resources, this strategy would be used to determine the optimal point of staffing.

The formula modification method is useful in cases where you have different rates based on the range of values. One of the best examples of this would be the computation of taxes. The U.S. tax structure is based on a sliding scale of profit. Based on the amount of profit, you would pay a different percentage of taxes. The computation of taxes on profit is a formula within the context of Multiplan. By careful analysis of capital expenditures, investment tax credits, and depreciation, you can examine alternatives which could be used to minimize your tax liabilities. The formula for computing tax liabilities can be modified to take into account all possible factors.

In the case of scientific analysis, you might set up Multiplan to calculate one of the more difficult problems: stress calculations. In this situation, you would have supports on a beam and you would be interested in the strains based on multiple weights placed on the surface of the beam. Using a what-if strategy, you can move weights along the beam to find the maximum point of stress. If you are working within the constraints of an existing stress bearing structure, you might use Multiplan to try out different arrangements of load to minimize stress. Again, the power of this package lies in its ability to allow you to try out different numbers and see the results of your choices—without destroying anything (building, company, organization or whatever).

Multiplan is even more useful than we have suggested, since you can do more than just look at the results—you can use the results in other reports. There are two ways in which you can use the results of Multiplan: printing and copying data.

When we prepare a spreadsheet using Multiplan on Mac we can insert titles over columns as well as rows. To round things out, we can also title the entire analysis. Using the print function, we can print out the entire spreadsheet on a printer attached to Mac. This form of output is called hard copy and is useful for presentation to accounting types, but we can go much further.

The ability to copy data between programs is one of the best things about Multiplan and the Mac. Using the mouse feature of the Mac we can select the entire spreadsheet (or even a portion) and transfer the data into another document (a letter for example) or another analysis tool—all without retyping the results. Consider the places in which we would like to use the results of Multiplan: analysis reports, quarterly statements, sales reports, mixed with charts, attached to pictures—the possibilities are limited by your imagination. The reason for a machine like Mac is its ability to move information without the need for programmers, manuals, and a great deal of confusion. In the case of Multiplan, if we want to move data to another program we simply put it on the Clipboard (see Chapter 7) and move to another program where we can pull it off the Clipboard—it's that simple. You control what goes on and off the Clipboard and all of the data is designed to be easily moved.

What then does Multiplan do for you? It provides a tireless servant who is more than happy to prepare reports based on information which you give it. Multiplan also is happy to try as many different approaches to this data as you like. Being a fantastic number cruncher and cooperative tool, it is happy to give the results to all of the other tools in Mac.

The operation of Mac, while easy, does involve a few new concepts which you should know about. After learning these new ideas, your first reaction will be "well of course, how else could you do all of that if you don't do it *that* way"; we will show you how to do things the MacMultiplan way next.

Starting up MacMultiplan

Multiplan is an optional tool which you will have to purchase for use on your Mac. The minimum requirements for running Multiplan are the Mac computer and the Multiplan disk. A printer is not required but is necessary if you would like to take the output of the Multiplan package away from Mac.

To start up Multiplan, turn on the power to Mac and insert the Multiplan disk (**Fig. 10-2**). You will notice a delay of approximately 30 seconds while the operating system and other packages are started up. You can view this time as the time needed to transfer the intelligence or instructions from the disk to the memory of Mac. Once Mac is loaded up, you will find the delays are significantly shorter—there is less to load from the disk of course.

Once you see the main display come on, select the Multiplan file with the mouse by pressing the button on the mouse while pointing to the folder or selection on the list (this will depend on whether the directory is being displayed as icons (**Fig. 10-3**) or listed by file name and qualifier). Now that you have the Multiplan file selected, go the the File menu on the top of the screen and press the button on the mouse and at the same time move the mouse down till the OPEN symbol is turned black (selected)—release the

Fig. 10-2   To start Multiplan, insert the Multiplan disk after power-on.

button now to start Multiplan. You should see the OPEN legend blink for about a second and the loading of Multiplan will proceed. The entire loading process of Multiplan should take about 20 seconds—while the loading is happening, you will see that screen get progressively more complete as it assembles the elements of Multiplan.

When Multiplan is loaded initially, the spreadsheet is totally clear of all information (**Fig. 10-4**). Let's examine what's on the screen.

What's in a Plan

In the topmost portion of the screen is the Mac System menu which we have seen on every screen produced by Mac. These selections are used to control the operation of Multiplan:

Apple logo—Supplies help information on Multiplan as well as the standard desk accessories.

File—Controls the loading and unloading of files for Multiplan. We also use this class to set up the page as well as print the spreadsheet. It also serves as our escape hatch to leave Multiplan.

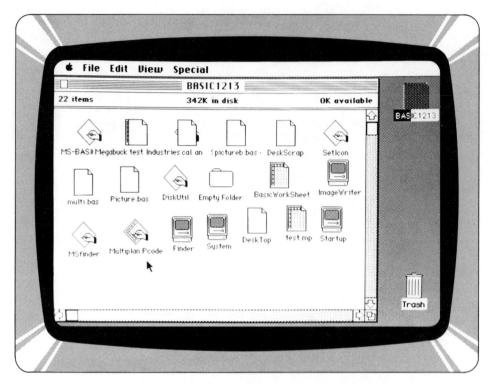

Fig. 10-3 Point to the Multiplan icon to select it.

Edit—Allows us to edit the contents of the spreadsheet as well as inter-acting with the Clipboard. We also use this selection to sort the spreadsheet.

Select—We would use this class of command when we wanted to format a cell (entry location) or all cells in the spreadsheet. Within this menu we can access a group of cells by name.

Format—Allows us to set up the cells in the spreadsheet for different types of data. We could, for example, set the number of decimal places, select display of dollar figures or even bar graphs. This section also allows us to set the size of the cells for holding numbers.

Options—Beyond what you normally would expect, this spreadsheet program has the ability to protect cells or groups of cells from being modified accidentally. We can also display either the results of calculations or the formulas which are responsible for the results. As you can probably realize, the cells are used to store both numbers you enter as well as the formulas which provide results. This command allows you to switch modes.

Calculate—Just having formulas and numbers is not enough. There are cases in which we have just entered a new formula and we want the spreadsheet to recalculate the results of our new formulas or data. This option is used to control the recalculation of the spreadsheet. Since you may

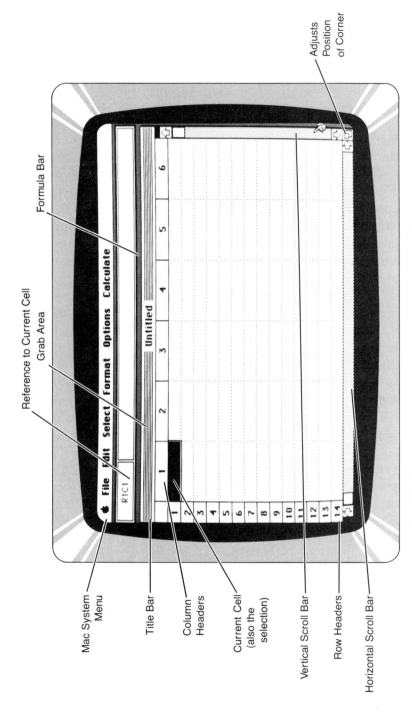

Fig. 10-4 These are the parts of a Multiplan display.

be interested in doing forms of regressive analysis, you can also control the stopping point of calculations. This *COMPLETION TEST* option allows you to set the minimum delta value which will cause termination of regression.

Now that we have examined the topmost portion of the screen, let's examine the spreadsheet area itself. The bar below the Mac menu is the *formula bar*, which is used to indicate the current position to enter data (numbers) or formulas. The left most reference box shows us the (R)ow and (C)olumn number of the *current cell*. The area to the right of the position location is the area in which we enter data and view data in the current cell. This area gives us a more complete display of the data we are entering—the cell itself is limited to the display of its width (default width is 10 characters). You will notice that when you enter information into this area, what you type is displayed in both the formula bar as well as in the current cell. The formula bar is also used to inspect the contents of the current cell. This is best illustrated by moving the cursor from cell to cell and pressing the button on the mouse to make the cell pointed to active. When you stop on a cell that has contents that are beyond the display capacity of the cell, you will see the *entire* cells' contents in the formula bar area.

Below the formula bar you will find the *title bar* which contains the name of the current spreadsheet. It is important at this point to explain the exact nature of a spreadsheet. The spreadsheet itself is really composed into numeric data, formulas, titles of rows and columns, and attributes such as protection and widths of fields. When saving a spreadsheet, what is being saved is not only the information about the situation you're analyzing—the number and formulas, that is—but the state in which Multiplan was set in to do your analysis. This information has to be retained so that your exit and entry to Multiplan would be as painless as possible—in other words: human engineering. That's what Mac is all about.

The title bar also has another interesting property: it is the point at which you grab hold of the spreadsheet and move it around. When you place the mouse pointer in this area, it will change into a cross with arrows pointing up, down, left, and right. If you then press and hold the mouse button, you will see a grid around the spreadsheet which you can move with the mouse. This outline represents the top left side of the spreadsheet. If you hold the button down and move it where you like, when you release the button, the spreadsheet will be redrawn in the position where you released the button. This illustrates the ability to move windows around. In other words, we can move the spreadsheet window wherever we like on the display screen. To put the window back in its normal position, you would place the pointer in the title bar plus press and hold the button on the mouse while you place the grid in the proper position. You should know that if you try to place the grid outline in an improper position and release the button, the window will remain in its current position.

Below the title bar are the *column headers* arranged across the screen (visibly from 1 to 6) which are used to indicate what current cell column you are in. You can think of these numbers as road signs that tell you what area of the spreadsheet you are in. There are a total of 63 columns in Multiplan. If you were doing a check register in which you were charging to different accounts, you would have a total of 63 accounts to which you could charge. Below each column you will see 14 visible rows of cells. The topmost cell is usually used to store the title of that particular column. In fact, we really have two pieces of information to deal with: the grid location (in this case 1 to 63) and the title of the column (which humans are more interested in). When you print out the spreadsheet you have the option of removing this external number information so that all that is printed is the actual information—not the supporting grid information.

On the left side of the screen you will see the *row headers* which map the row locations currently visible on the screen. There are a total of 255 rows of which only 14 can be displayed at a time. As with the columns, we normally reserve the leftmost cell for the title of the row. We would use the 255 rows to hold the more numerous entries.

At this point we know what we have is a large piece of ledger paper that is composed of 63 columns across and 255 rows down, but what would we use this for? An example might be an analysis by state in the U.S. of each of 250 items in a sales inventory. We would assign each state (50) to a column. We would then assign each product to a row. What we now have is a heck of a lot of information, but what do we do with it now.?

There is simple and complex analysis. The simplest analysis is to put a formula and title at the end of every last column and row indicating the totals per product, and per state. This is good, but we can do even better. Let's say you are the sales manager of a company and you feel that certain states are a total loss—fine decision, since no amount of juggling will help some situations. You do have a feeling that certain states could be profitable if only you could sell only those products which generated a substantial enough return for the effort. In other words, you are looking for the optimum product mix for each state. You can do this with Multiplan. The method is simple: you simply put in different formulas (more than 1) that sum sales per state using different product mixes. You can take this one step further and use the cost information per state to determine which strategies yield better than break-even—and by how much. We will discuss how to write such formulas a little bit later in this chapter.

There are only a few more things left on the screen to discuss, and those are the scroll bars. Remember when we mentioned that there were 63 by 255 different cells on our spreadsheet? You may be wondering how, with only 6 by 14 being displayed, we get to these other cells. The answer is we use the scroll bars.

What are scroll bars anyway? Consider for a moment what our screen really is capable of doing. Since we have so many elements in the computer, and such a limited display, what we need to do is only show a portion of the entire set of information. To get to the other pieces of information in our Mac, we need to roll off (scroll off) the information being currently displayed and roll in (scroll in) the proper area of information. The best analogy would be that of having a black piece of paper with a square cut in the center of it. If we placed this piece of paper with the hole in it over the page of a newspaper, we would be only able to read a portion of the newspaper. To read further, we would have to move the paper down or around. The control over this window into our information is by two scroll bars: one for vertical scrolling and the other for horizontal scrolling.

The horizontal scroll bar is located at the bottom of the screen. Notice the two arrows at the bottom: one pointing left and the other right. Also notice that between these arrows is a white box. This white box represents the window's position relative to the entire array of 63 columns. To move our window, we move our mouse to one of the arrows and press the button on the mouse. Notice that when we press the button the white box moves and, at the same time, the column numbers have changed. If we had information on the screen, it too was moved. An interesting feature is that if we hold the button down the window will begin to move continuously. We all know you are busy, and certainly you don't have time to wait for your data to scroll, so we have an easier way. If you place the pointer right on the box and press and hold the button, when you move the mouse horizontally you will see an outline move across the scroll bar. This outline represents the final position of the window with respect to the beginning and end of the scrollable area (marked by the left and right arrows). You can, by this method, move the window wherever you like almost instantly. Pretty clever!

Not to be outdone by the horizontal scroll bar, the vertical scroll bar can do exactly the same thing, only vertically. The scroll bar is located on the far right edge of the screen and has two arrows: up and down, which indicate the beginning and end of the scrollable area. Notice also that there is a white box located between the two arrows, indicating our window's position.

The final feature shown in the display is the small square located in the bottom rightmost part of the screen. If you examine it very closely you might see what looks like two boxes in it. This box allows us to move the display of Multiplan by its rightmost bottom corner. To move the display, put the mouse pointer in the box (it will change to a cross with arrows on all four corners) and press and hold the button on the mouse. You can now move the mouse and see the outline of the Multiplan area move. When you release the button, and if the corner is in a valid area, the entire Multiplan display will be offset into your new position.

Now that we have described what the screen looks like and how we move from area to area, let's now concentrate on the techniques of actually using MacMultiplan.

If You Can't Put It in Numbers, It's Not Real

To enter information in a cell, select the cell, type the information, and press the ENTER key. The information also appears in the formula bar as you type. Information can be text, numbers or formulas. One cell can hold up to 255 characters.

Multiplan automatically aligns text to the left and numbers to the right in a cell. You can change the alignment with the *ALIGN RIGHT*, *ALIGN CENTER*, or *ALIGN LEFT COMMANDS* (**Fig. 10-5**).

Your text can include letters, numbers or printable characters. You can consider anything that MacMultiplan cannot interpret as a number as being text or a formula.

If the text you type is too long to fit into the single cell you started in, the next cell will be used for display. The only exception to this rule is if the

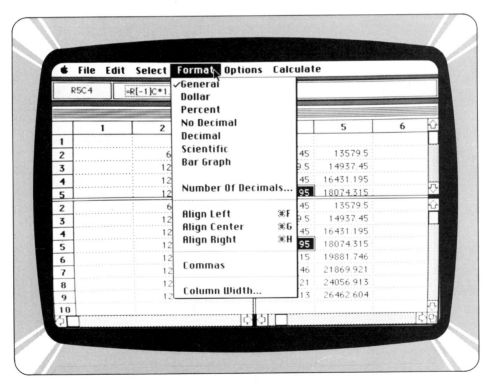

Fig. 10-5   The format menu contains a multitude of commands to change a cell's format.

adjacent cell already contains information. In the case of an adjacent cell, only that portion which can be display will be—but the entire text is stored within the machine internally. No data is lost.

There are cases in which you would like to store numbers as text as in the case of the year. In this case, you would place the number in ditto marks ("1984"). Whatever is placed in ditto marks is interpreted as text.

MacMultiplan can understand quite a range of numbers from scientific notation to decimal numbers (**Fig. 10-6**). Its three principal modes of storage are:

- Integers (Example: 1023, −9, 14)
- Decimal fractions (Example: 12.87, −16.2, 15.55)
- Scientific notation (Examples: 1.25E15, 6.02E23, 1.03E-31)

Multiplan interprets the following characters as part of numbers:

$$1\ 2\ 3\ 4\ 5\ 6\ 7\ 8\ 9\ 0\ -\ +\ .\ E\ e$$

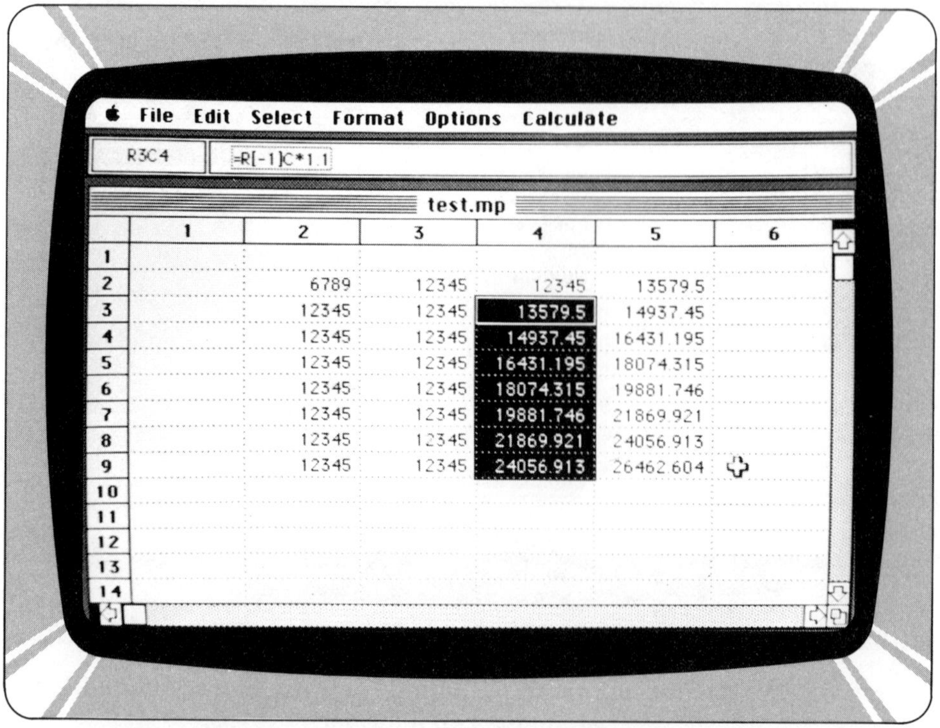

Fig. 10-6 **Multiplan accepts a wide variety of numbers.**

When you are displaying numbers, the number displayed depends on the format specified for that cell. If the number exceeds the width (or capacity) of a cell, then the cell is filled with the number sign characters:

$$#######$$

The largest number that MacMultiplan can accept is:

$$9.9999999999999 \times 10^{62}$$

The smallest number that MacMultiplan can accept is:

$$0.1 \times 10^{-64}$$

If you enter a number either smaller than the minimum, or greater than the maximum, Multiplan will treat it as text.

One of the most important capabilities of Multiplan is its ability to display numbers in different formats. There is the potential for confusion however. This stems from the belief that what you see displayed in a cell is all that is kept there. Let me try to explain this a bit. There are two formats possible for any number. The first format is the internal format which stores and calculates all numbers to the maximum amount of precision possible by Multiplan. The second format is that which is used to display numbers. The display format is designated by the format specification of the display cell. This specification can be changed by pulling down the Format selection in the Mac menu and changing the selection for the current cell or cells. The available number formats are:

- General—default format
- Dollar—display quantities with dollar and cents
- Percent—display as percentages
- No Decimal—no decimal display
- Scientific—show numbers in scientific notation
- Bar Graph—graphic display of quantity in cell

A Formula for Everything

You use formulas to calculate a new value from existing values. A formula can contain numbers, text, references to other cells on the worksheet, names, operators, or functions. You can have formulas as simple as = R1C1 + R1C2, which adds the contents of cells R1C1 to that of R1C2 and places the result in the cell containing the formula. The notation R1C1 stands for the cell located at (R)ow (1) (C)olumn (1).

Another capability which is unique to MacMultiplan is its ability to mark groups of cells with a name. By marking cells with a name, you can insert the entire group by using its name—quite a time saver.

If you look at our simple equation, you probably noticed that it starts with an equal sign. This indicates to Multiplan that you are about to enter information which will create a formula. As an added convenience, once a current cell has been selected and the " = " sign has been entered, you may select cells that are to be used for summation. This is done by placing the mouse at each cell and pressing the mouse button—the location of the cell selected will be appended to the current formula with a plus sign. When you have included all of the cells needed for a summation, press the ENTER key. It is important to note that the formula that is being created is designed to use whatever is contained within the cells specified. If you change the value in a cell that is referenced by a formula, the formula will normally recalculate the new total for that formula.

When reviewing the formulas produced by this mouse selection process, you may have noticed that rather than inserting the absolute label of the cells being added, such as R1C5, it instead used a value like R[-3]C. This is what is known as reference by *relative offset from the current cell.* In the case of R[− 3]C, we are referring to the cell which is located 3 rows above the current cell in the same column (**Fig. 10-7**).

Relative references are important when we are interested in copying the formulas from one area to another. By using relative references, a formula transported from one column to another will always work if the *relative* locations are still valid. This assumption is usually true when working with columnar data with equal numbers of rows.

If all we could do was add, the versatility of MacMultiplan would be quite limited. Fortunately, MacMultiplan has a rich variety of operations on three groups of data:

- Arithmetic
- Text
- Comparison

With *arithmetic operators* we can perform the following operations on numbers:

+	Addition
−	Subtraction
*	Multiplication
/	Division
%	Percent
^	Exponentiation

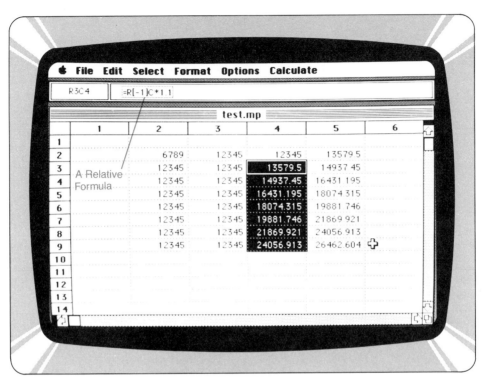

Fig. 10-7 **The formula bar displays the relative formula of the current cell.**

On *text* we can perform *concatenation* (attaching groups of text together) on strings of text. An example would be the concatenation of "Howard" & "Sams" would produce a single text result of "Howard Sams."

We can also perform comparisons which will tell us if conditions of the equations are either true or false. The following logical comparisons can be performed:

=	Equal
<	Less than
<=	Less than or equal
>	Greater than
>=	Greater than or equal
<>	Not equal

Special Effects I—Multiple Windows

As we have seen, the capabilities of MacMultiplan are quite extensive and comprehensive. There are a few more features that just seem to round out the package, and make it the polished piece of work it is.

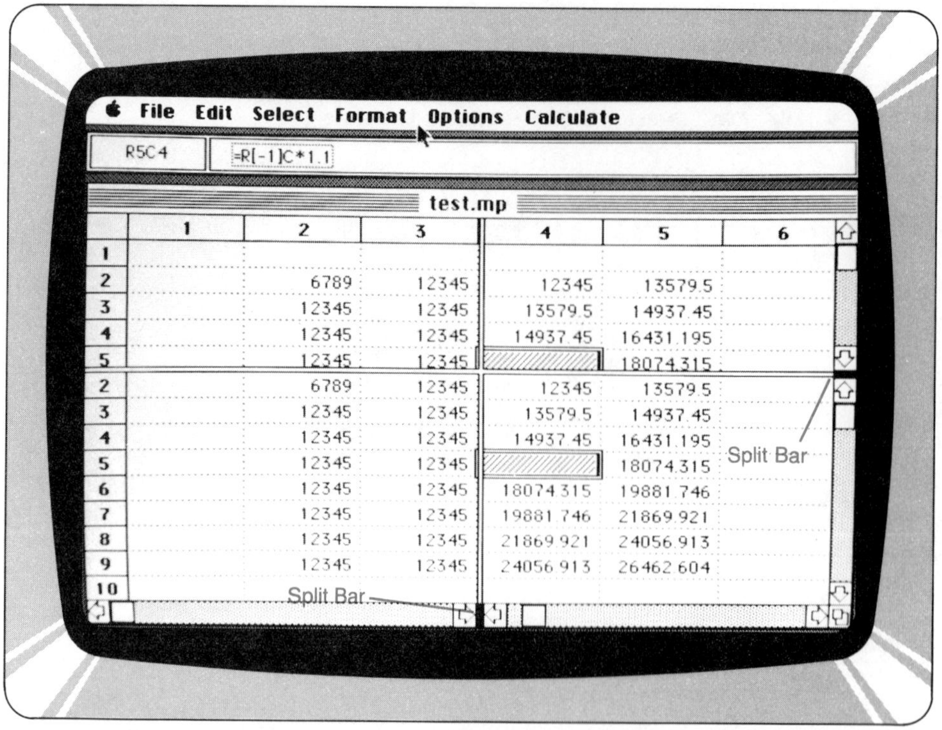

Fig. 10-8   The split bars allows the screen to be divided into 4 quadrants which can be scrolled independently.

When we described the display screen, we neglected to mention two small rectangular bars: one horizontal bar, located in the upper right top side of the screen; the other, a vertical bar, located in the lower left bottom area of the screen. These two bars perform a quite remarkable feat: they allow you to split up the spreadsheet into multiple windows which can be scrolled independently (**Fig. 10-8**).

To split the spreadsheet into a top and bottom half, we move the mouse pointer to the black bar located in the upper right top of the screen and press and hold the button on the mouse. We then pull the mouse down, at which time we see a bar appear across the screen which moves down as we pull the mouse. This bar represents where the screen will be split when we release the button. Once you have the bar positioned at the center of the screen, release the button. The result will be two copies of the top rows of the spreadsheet. Notice also that there are now two sets of scroll bars on the screen—one for each new window.

If we wanted to scroll horizontally, we would place the mouse pointer at the bar located at the bottom left portion of the screen and press and hold the mouse button. While holding the button, move the mouse to the right and observe how a bar begins to move across the screen. To split the screen in half, move the bar to the center and release the button. Notice we now have 4 sets of scroll bars—pretty amazing, we think.

To restore the original windows, we position the pointer on the new black bar position and put it back into the appropriate place.

Special Effects II—Frozen Titles

In cases where you have a very large spreadsheet and there is a tendency for the titles to scroll off, you may wish to lock the titles into place. Mac-Multiplan will even put this in for you. To freeze titles, select a cell below and to the right of the titles to be frozen. Next, choose the *FREEZE TITLE* command from the Options menu. The titles that are frozen are dependent on the cell you select. The rule is that all cells that are located above and to the left of the selected cell are frozen in place. The effect of a frozen title is that the row and column headings are always there, no matter where we scroll in the spreadsheet.

Even More

We can't hope to tell you about all of the terrific features that Mac-Multiplan offers in this limited space. We recommend that you purchase the package and let your imagination run wild.

The capability of linking worksheets, protecting areas, iteration, conditional branching will be left for you, the Mac user, to discover—we don't think you'll be disappointed.

THE ELEVENTH CHAPTER

More Software

MultiTools Are Available Too • Even More Is Adapted

A Taste of What's Available • Put Your Life in Order

Report Supports File • Use Your Imagination

Along the Tree Branch

More Software

Beyond MacPaint and MacWrite (discussed in Chapters 6 and 7, respectively) from Apple, a mountain of software is rapidly becoming available from additional sources. Many of the programs include software originally written for other computers and now adapted for Macintosh.

Among these programs are Microsoft's popular *Multitools series*, including BASIC, which they dub *MacBASIC*, discussed in Chapter 9, and a special enhanced version of Multiplan called *MacPlan* (see Chapter 10).

If you have had previous experience with Multiplan using other computer systems, then you are aware of the powerful functions that are possible with this popular program. You already know that not only is it easy to use, but complex spreadsheets can be created. By being enhanced for use on the Macintosh, and with the MacMouse, the software is even more powerful. Moreover, it permits the creation of graphs to further illustrate a given set of calculations.

MultiTools Are Available Too

Besides the programs mentioned so far, you will soon be able to add the rest of the MultiTools, including the Microsoft *WORD*, to your Macintosh. Howard W. Sams publishes books on these products too.

But there are other packages as well. For example, programs that are recast for the Macintosh graphics-based user interface now take on new depth and suggest future approaches.

One consideration with the use of icons rather than words and numbers, however, is that for any object or operation to be represented, a new icon must be created. Of course, words and numbers can be applied endlessly without stretching an imagination out of shape. The sparks really have to fly across the synapses to dream up collections of apt graphic metaphors that fit a conventional program application to the Macintosh environment.

Even More Is Adapted

You will recognize many of the independent third party software suppliers in this list. Dozens more are hard at work adapting popular programs and cooking up new software for Macintosh.

At this point, you know about two programs from Microsoft that are ready to go. Among the many companies developing software for Mac are:

- Software Publishing Corp., Mountain View, CA
- Lotus Development Corp., Cambridge, MA
- Hayden Software, Lowell, MA
- DB Master Associates, Flourtown, PA

And of course Howard W. Sams & Co., Inc., is on the list with a full list of business and engineering software tools.

A Taste of What's Available

Lotus Development is offering a version of the popular *Lotus 1-2-3* package, greatly enhanced for use with the Macintosh special functions. This package, if you're unfamiliar with it, combines a simple word processing program, a spreadsheet, and a data base manager. Interestingly, unlike the Microsoft products or Apple packages, the files aren't compatible with other software tools.

For the game buffs, Hayden Software has adapted a version of the challenging chess game program, *Sargon III*. Although the versions for other systems were quite excellent, the Mac version is superb. Not only do you get the action of championship chess, but the movements on the board are as realistic as those on a real chessboard.

Even though games are important and Hayden, Sams, and other publishers are offering a large store to choose from, business is one of the more important areas for the Mac. As a result, other companies, such as DB Master, has an easy-to-use and simple data base management package that works with the MacMouse and employs windows to keep track of inventory and other reference material. In addition, Ashton-Tate has a version of *dBase III* that is designed to work in concert with the Microsoft MultiTools, thus turning the Macintosh into an extremely powerful workstation. This, coupled with the ability to communicate to the IBM mainframe world, turns the Mac into a limitless information machine.

In addition to the above mentioned products, you can look for software from:

- Continental Software, Los Angeles, CA
- Think Technologies, Danvers, MA
- Tecmar, Inc., Cleveland, OH
- SORCIM, San Jose, CA
- Living Videotext, Inc., Palo Alto, CA

All the programs employ the use of icons and work with the mouse and keyboard. The idea of Mac is to maintain as much compatibility as possible.

Two other significant programs that found favor among Apple II users are: *PFS:File* and *PFS:Report* from Software Publishing in Mountain View, CA. As are other programs, these have also been rewritten for the MacWorld.

Put Your Life in Order

The PFS:File program turns Mac into a personal filing system. Unlike many other data handling systems, this program is designed to operate at the lowest possible level yet provide the means for storing and retrieving information according to categories you stipulate. Coupled with the Mac, their operation becomes even that much easier.

In operation, PFS:Files are arranged in accordance with forms that you design. Related information is categorized within a file as you please, and can be called up from storage by citing various qualifying parameters of your choice. For example, you can create a personnel record form. Such a form can describe employees by name, employee number, address, job title, salary, and date of employment. By using data from your company workforce file, you can relate separate entries in any way you please.

For example, you might want to distribute champagne to all employees on their anniversaries with the company. You can find out who was hired on any particular date. If you want to know which employees with names that begin with the letter S earn more than $40,000 a year, you can do that too. The software is arranged in such a way as to allow the definition of data in very human ways. This coupled with Mac's display functions means that more than one attribute can be displayed at a time, and overlapping windows can be employed for comparison.

Information you request can be displayed on the MacScreen or printed for prolonged scrutiny. You might not care to spend more than an instant reviewing who, with the initial S, you can borrow money from, but you very well might want a permanent calendar of toasts.

The design file function of PFS:File lets you create a new file or make alterations to the forms of an old one, even if the old file contains data. With a function called *add*, you store information as forms in the file. A *copy* function duplicates file forms, selected forms *filled-in* with information, or entire files. Data is retrieved by the search and update function. For spring cleaning, the "remove" function cleans forms from a file.

Files for information are created with the *design file* function. Incidentally, the auxiliary external microfloppy disk drive is *mandatory* to enjoy benefits from the PFS:File program. You get a disk to hold a file, name the file, design a form, and store the form in the file. Once the file is created, you can refer to it by name, and use the form to store information in it, and retrieve information from it.

When you design a form, you determine how to arrange the information you want to retain. You pick names to label categories of data. You must estimate the space required on a form to accommodate information in each category. For efficient retrieval of information, the most sought data should be the first item on a form.

Once a file is created, the add function stores information within it. Forms are added to a file in any order you please.

To conduct a search for a form, you indicate the information you want on a retrieval specification. Only those forms in a file that meet all the criteria you stipulate are gathered. There are several methods available to conduct a search, based on whether you have a specific, or a general idea of what you want.

The fact that anything that can retrieved from files and printed according to your specification suggests wonderful possibilities.

Report Supports File

The PFS:Report program for Mac enables you to tabulate data from files created with the PFS:File program. The tabular reports produced by the programs can have up to nine vertical columns. The layout of a report is automatically arranged to make the best use of available space. Information can be sorted alphabetically or numerically, and the program can make calculations on numerical information.

The process of retrieving information for reports works much the same way as extracting forms for display in PFS:File. Selections can be limited to specific entries or generalized. The program gives you a lot of latitude to determine the format of a report to be printed.

Interestingly, because both the Macintosh and the Imagewriter printers are capable of producing high-quality graphics, you can elect to use this capability in developing reports. By using the report design functions found in the software, coupled with the functions of MacWrite and MacPaint, you can design very unusual and spectacular reports.

Use Your Imagination

Given the information in the employee file example, you could print out an address list for holiday greetings, for example. Or, if you wish, print a profile of employee age, company experience, and salary.

Updated reports for inventory control are a fine example of how the programs can be applied to improve your productivity and profit. For scholastic courses, your efficiency at collecting, filing and finding notes can be increased by orders of magnitude.

APPENDIX A

The Soul of the Macintosh

What is this strange beast called a microprocessor? Well, we could give you the standard engineering lingo of instruction sets and addressing modes—but if you are like me, you will be unconscious (eyes rolled back in your head) within 30 seconds. Instead, let me tell you some of the miraculous things that the microprocessor contained within your Macintosh can do for you.

First off, what shall we call this beast that does all of the work for you? Its official title is a Motorola 68000—for those of you who would like to impress your friends with your engineering and scientific acumen, you can refer to it as the Motorola 68K ("sixty-eight kay"). Now that you know what it's called, what other things are significant about it?

Remember the Apple II, that standard of the personal computer field? It's a great machine but there were a few things which could drive you right up the wall. Its biggest limitation was the limited amount of memory in it. Memory, I don't know anything about memory you say . . . but wait. If you are a user of any sort of spreadsheet program that runs on the Apple II (or other small personal computer), you have undoubtedly run into the problems of having too much information for your spreadsheet. Perhaps you are thinking, "I use my computer for different things—memory is not the problem, it's those slow disks that keep grinding away." Interestingly enough, all of that activity with your disks is related to the computer's lack of sufficient memory.

What is this thing called memory anyway? Memory is really a conglomeration of chips inside your computer that holds the program and data you are using. Here is the trick—the more memory you have, the less often the computer has to go out to its disks to get information. What the computer would like to do is have all of its program and data in memory at the same time—not spread out—some on disk; some in memory. Imagine how much work your computer goes through when you ask for information that is not in memory. So why not just put more memory into our Apple II or other personal computer? The answer is: the microprocessor can't handle it. The first generation of personal computers used what are known as 8-bit micro-processors. These simple machines, while very capable, cannot deal effectively with more than 65,536 elements of information (bytes). That seems like a very large number of locations—and it is. What has happened is quite interesting: programs and data originally intended for these simple 8-bit machines have grown and grown . . . till the combination of large amounts of data and complex programs finally swamped these first generation machines—and brought about the birth of Macintosh.

This first lack of horsepower by these 8-bit machines has been corrected in the MacEngine (68000) used by Apple in its Macintosh. In fact, this new processor can use over 256 *times* as much memory effectively—16,777,216 bytes (16 megabytes). Quite a jump, you're thinking, but why so much of a jump when these first generation computers were "just barely running out of space"? This memory is used to hold the beauty and elegance of the Macintosh: its stunning graphics; helpful and comprehensive menus; and a large base of information available at your fingertips. This vast area of memory is used by Macintosh to perform the magic you see.

Having a lot of memory to work with is very handy in presenting information, but what about grinding that information down into results we can use? This is the second area in which that MacEngine acts like a drag racer—computational ability. You probably don't want to hear about bits, nibbles, bytes, words and long words. In fact these measures of data size really affect the performance quite a bit. Rather than discuss all of the attributes of each of these data elements, let's just define the significant differences. The first generation personal computers dealt with bytes (a data element containing 8 bits). The microprocessor in the Macintosh deals with long words (a data element with 32 bits). Because your Macintosh microprocessor deals with data elements that are so much bigger (32 bits/8 bits = 4 times bigger), it's capable of working with more and bigger numbers than its 8-bit small brother.

Up to this point we have talked about the increased memory size and the 68000's ability to deal with larger pieces of data, but we have not talked about the speed of the microprocessor. To better understand what speed means to a microprocessor, we can make an analogy between a computer and a racing car on speeding down a race track. We can consider the length of the track to be the addressing range of the microprocessor (16 megabytes)—the longer the track, the more interesting the race. The width of the track would correspond to the size of data handled by the microprocessor (32 bits)—the wider the track, the more cars in the race. Finally, the speed of the car and the skill of the driver can be measured by the clock speed and instruction efficiency of the processor—a measure of what operations the machine can perform, and how well it performs those same operations.

To give you a "feel" for the relative speed of operations done in those simple first generation personal computers, we can first compare the speed of the master clock which serves as the "heartbeat" of the micro. The faster this clock, the faster the machine will complete its tasks. This translates into faster computations as well as zippier response to requests for information. The clock that is running in the Macintosh runs at 7,833,600 cycles-per-second. This means the internal operation of the 68000 microprocessor in the Macintosh is performing operations internally at the rate of almost 8 million operations a second! Compare this to the frequency of the clock feeding the Apple II which is about 1,000,000 cycles-per-second. We see that the Macintosh runs at almost 8 times the speed.

If all this were not enough, the Macintosh MacEngine also can perform such operations as multiplication and division. The less sophisticated 8-bit microprocessors can do multiplication and division but only by simulation, which is slow and consumes space in the program.

Architecture of the MacEngine

For those who are interested in the "nitty-gritty" details of the 68000, we can tell you that it is a 16-bit microprocessor incorporating a 16-bit bus with 32-bit registers. The registers are split into two main groups: data registers and address registers. Both the data and address registers are 32 bits in size (**Fig. A-1**).

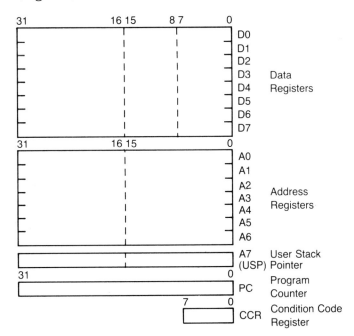

Fig. A-1   **Programmer's model of the 68000.**

The eight (8) data registers (called D0 . . D7) are designed to perform all mathematical functions and to act as general purpose accumulators. Data registers are used for all mathematical operations. Their 32 bit width makes them convenient for performing math on data types from bits to long words (32 bit quantities).

The address registers are designed to function as index registers—acting as pointers into memory. The address registers are limited in their mathematical capabilities—capable of incrementing and decrementing only. To their defense, these address registers can autoincrement or autodecrement. This automatic adjustment of the register value may be applied before or after the register is used (pre- vs. post-fix operation). Further enhancing the power of the address registers is the ability to perform "double-address" operations such as "move indirect from register A1 to indirect register A2 with autoincrement on both registers." These sorts of operations are similar to those performed in the Digital Equipment Corporation PDP-11™ (which the 68000 was modeled after).

A further enhancement of the state-of-the-art in microprocessor design is the 68000's more logical implementation of instructions. We can say that a programmer of the 68000 will find the instructions (also called an orthogonal instruction set) and programming of the machine more logical or regular.

High-Level Language

All of the features described so far point to a machine which is immensely more powerful than the processors being used in first generation microprocessors. They are faster, handle larger amounts of data, can process it faster, and are generally easier to program.

By virtue of their enhanced design (or architecture) they can effectively be used for writing programs. When you write a program in any language (FORTRAN, PASCAL, C, FORTH, etc.) the microprocessor must translate your English-like instructions into its native language, called assembly language. In the early generation personal computers which used 8-bit microprocessors, programs written in a high-level language would have two common characteristics: they were large and slow. Both of these characteristics came from the 8-bit processor's less sophisticated architecture. The processor used in the Macintosh does not have any of these limitations. Because of its enhanced architecture, it is capable of translating these high-level language programs into compact and fast assembly programs which run very efficiently.

Because it is possible (and easier) to write programs in these high-level languages (rather than in assembly language), we will see more sophisticated programs appear at a faster rate than in the 8-bit world. These same programs will have more features and be more reliable than was ever possible with the previous generation. The most exciting possibility that this transition to high-level languages will bring is portability.

We have now reached the crux of why the microprocessor in the Macintosh is so important. It relates to the fact that when a program is written in assembly language it is tied to that processor. Whether that processor is a 68000 or any other processor, the software written (if assembly language) is not transportable to any other type processor. Because of this, firms must feel that they will be able to receive enough return on their investment on that single type machine to justify the research and development needed. What programming in high-level language allows us to do is to take programs (say, written in PASCAL) which might be written for an IBM computer, and, in its existing form, compile it (change it to assembly language from high-level language), and have it run on our machine.

The ability to run high-level language in a microprocessor opens the vistas of software writers so that they can receive the benefits of having their software running on many different machines based on different microprocessors. The processor in the Macintosh (68000) supports such strategy superbly.

APPENDIX B

MacMouse's Innards

The MacMouse, whose operation we described in Chapter 3, is an ingenious animal.

Like the small furry animal that you may be thinking of, it runs around, is inquisitive and, most important, is small. All these attributes make the mouse friendly and something you would like to have around.

But the mouse that your Mac uses is even more interesting. This mouse is used as a pointing device, a paint brush, a pencil and even a spray can.

Surprisingly, the mouse is easy to use, as you found in previous chapters. Moreover, the mouse is an important part of Mac's operation.

Very Simple

Mouses can be very complex and require special grid patterns to function. This type of mouse is called an optical mouse, and isn't as flexible, or for that matter, as easy to use as MacMouse.

The MacMouse is called a mechanical mouse for very good reasons. It uses, as shown in the nearby photograph (**Fig. B-1**), a roller ball, and optical transducers that, with the help of electronics and software in the Mac, equate the relative position of the mouse to an actual location on the screen. By these means, you are able to roam around the screen, and through various windows.

The system hardware keeps track of the current position of the mouse. The MacEngine continually keeps track of the position of the mouse and displays a cursor (marker) on the screen to indicate where it is.

The MacMouse also has a button that is used to perform specific actions. For example, if you want to choose a menu item, you move the pointer over it and click the button on the mouse. As you have found, several actions can take place depending on what level you happen to be at.

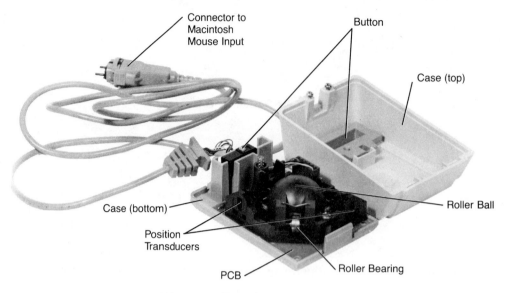

Fig. B-1 **Interior of mouse.**

You also found that holding the button down can turn the mouse pointer into a pencil, or brush, and that you can use it much like a spray can of paint. Further, it works as an eraser to remove whatever you did.

Tiny Resolution

One of the factors that makes the use of a mouse ideal is that it has what is termed pixel or bit resolution. Simply stated, that means that each dot available on the screen can be physically reached by moving the mouse pointer to it. As a result, you can draw pictures and create special designs.

APPENDIX C

The MacDisk

The MacDisk is more than just a storage device, but is representative of the harvesting of available technology that Apple is so good at doing.

Unlike other disk drives typically found on microcomputer systems, the MacDisk is less that 5-1/4-inches in diameter; thus, the drive, **Fig. C-1**, can be mounted into a very small space. Moreover, it employs a microprocessor that is used for translating the commands from the computer into useful functions on the disk drive.

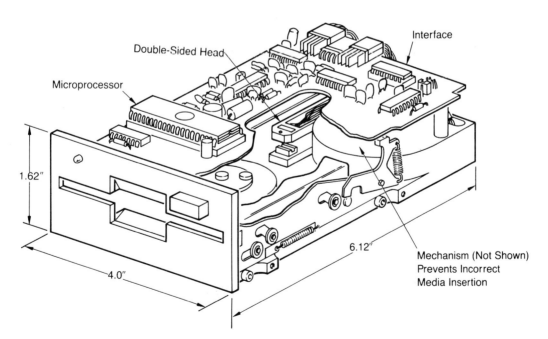

Fig. C-1 **Measuring 4 inches wide, the Mac's disk drive matches the computer's small size.**

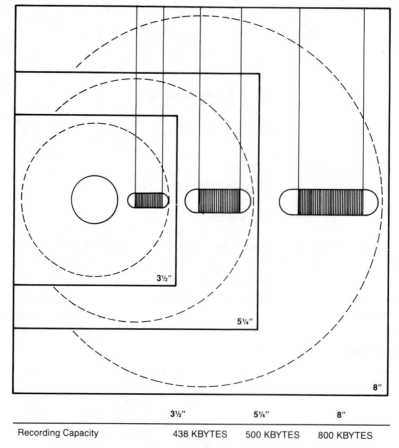

	3½"	5¼"	8"
Recording Capacity	438 KBYTES	500 KBYTES	800 KBYTES

Fig. C-2 **The small disk stores over 400,000 characters of information.**

Since the overall size of the disk drive is reduced, it is obvious that the actual disk (media) would be smaller. The media for the MacDrive, which incidentally is made by Sony Corp., uses a flexible disk that is 3 1/2 inches in diameter (**Fig. C-2**). As shown, the disk may be small, but it compares favorably with larger disks in terms of actual recording capacity. Notice that the 3 1/2 inch disk is capable of storing up to 438 kilobytes (448,512 characters) of information, which is slightly less than the much larger 5 1/4 inch package.

The 438 kilobytes is termed unformatted capacity. This simply means that this is the maximum amount of information that can be packed onto

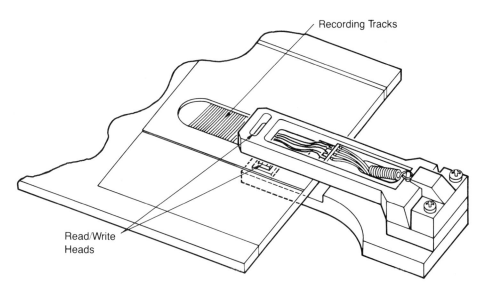

Recording Tracks

Read/Write
Heads

Fig. C-3   Adding an extra read/write head doubles capacity.

Manual Diskette Release

**Fig. C-4   A pinhole release mechanism lets you
manually eject the disk.**

the disk. However, this is trimmed down to about 400 kilobytes when the disk is formatted.

The formatting process is a function that sets the disk up to record information in a specific fashion. During formatting, it lays out the tracks and divides them into sectors—recording zones. It is within these recording zones that information is placed in a specific order so that it can be found readily. This formatting process, however, takes up storage space, but is critical to the operation of the drive.

The drive that is currently in the Macintosh is called a single-sided drive. Thus, information is only recorded on one side of the media. However, the capacity can be increased by recording information on the other side (a total of one million characters) as well, as shown in **Fig. C-3**. This greater capacity drive is available with the optional disk drive.

You have probably noticed that the disk used with the MacDrive differs from other disks in more than size. The media is packaged in a hard plastic case with a sliding metal window. This not only allows easier handling of the media, but prevents damage.

Apple has extended the capability of the small drive by making it easy to insert and remove the disk. On inserting the disk into the drive, it is automatically mounted. As you have learned in previous chapters, Mac can return the disk to you when it has finished with it.

There are times when you have to remove the disk manually. This is accomplished by inserting a small pin (such as paper clip) into the hole immediately to the right of the disk (**Fig. C-4**).

APPENDIX D

Friendly Utilities

Care and Feeding of Your Disks

As with many things in life, there is often some dirty work. In the case of owning a personal computer, you have to attend to the care and feeding of your machine. This appendix will explain what you need to know to keep your machine from becoming an unmanageable monster.

Foremost is the care and handling of disks. Even though the disks used by Mac are specially constructed to withstand punishment, they can still be damaged. The result can be a lobotomy of Macintosh's brain.

You know that dust and dirt are the worst enemies of disks. Since the media is covered, this is really not a significant problem. If, however, you open up the disk by pulling back the protective shutter, you'll find that the disk's surface is exposed and can be damaged.

One of the more interesting stories about disk care relates to an incident where a defective disk was inserted into a good drive. The defective disk damaged the drive permanently, but was unknown to the user who installed good disk after good disk. The effect was the transformation of good disks into bad. The point is to exercise care.

You, of course, aren't the inquisitive and destructive type so you won't open the covered disks. Thus, you will have nothing to worry about, right? Wrong! Some of the most destructive effects are invisible and can take place with all of the covers on the disk in place. We are, of course referring to magnetic fields.

Well, wait a minute, I don't't have any magnets you say; but let's look at some of the culprits. The prime agents of destruction are probably desk accessories which have magnets in them. A clock radio (something with a speaker), a television set or monitor, telephone, and yes, even a desk light.

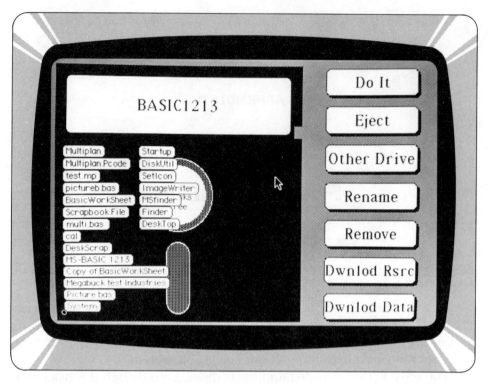

Fig. D-1   Utility Menu.

All these devices have magnetic fields about them. Since all of your precious data as well as the tools for your work are stored as magnetic patterns on the disk, a new source of magnetism can cause the data on your disk to be zapped—permanently.

Perhaps one of the most surprising methods of disk destruction is by temperature. It is not unusual for people to leave disks in direct sunlight. This can be a severe problem since the case may warp (even melt) leaving your data reorganized into a pool of melted plastic.

Disk care goes even to the original purchase of disks. There are many factors which influence the selections of brand of disks—one of these factors should not be price. There are no bargains! You may not be aware of it, but disks have limited lifetimes and wear out. The cause of wear is simple: constant contact of the read/write head with the surface of the disk media. This situation can best be illustrated by a tire which eventually becomes bald and then . . . BLOW OUT! This same scenario can happen to your disks, but there are no jacks and spare tires to speed you off with a minor inconvenience. You have to plan for a blow out by making copies of your disks *regularly.*

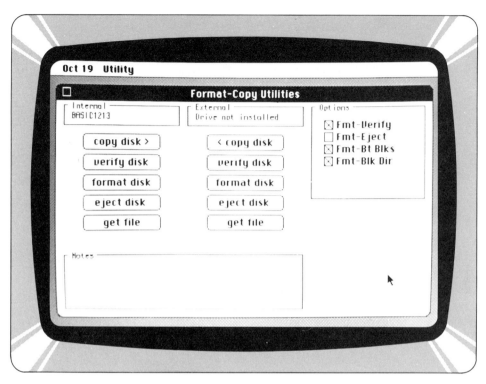

Fig. D-2   Format Copy Utilities.

Buying Insurance

The question is not whether your disks will go bad, but when. Since the people at Apple realize that you have to make copies of your disks, they provide a way to do this on the disks you receive with your machine. If you want to make copies of your disks (backups), refer to your owner's manual for the appropriate commands. You will be using this operation quite frequently.

We would suggest that you review the actual operation of the copy procedure before using your Mac for the first time. Failure to do so may result in some nasty consequences. But if you do follow all of the rules, your Mac will be like a good friend—always predictable, and ready to make you the ultimate knowledge worker of the 80's.

MacGlossary

Much earlier in this book, we explained that you would learn new words, concepts and phrases. Now that you have gotten this far, almost the end of the book, you have run into just about every one of these words and ideas. In some cases, you probably found that the words weren't really new, but how they were used was foreign to the way you think about them.

Well don't be upset, just a short nine years ago personal computers were foreign to everyone. Now they are everywhere. And with the creation of Macintosh, a new era is upon us.

So that we can both continue to enjoy the experience of Macintosh and further explore the magic of the machine and concept, we've decided to dispense with the normal way of doing a glossary. Rather, we will explore the words and put them in context to the book, you and, of course, our friend the Macintosh.

If you're expecting to find these words in alphabetical order, you're in for a surprise. You don't necessarily work in a directly ordered fashion, and as far as anyone can tell, few people, if any, think in a sequential, ordered way. Therefore, we'll take the words, and concepts, in the order that you will probably think of them. You can assume this is the haphazard way we think; but, surprisingly, we can usually muddle our way through.

From the Ground up

Even though we're not looking at these words in a normal order, they are in order just the same. And because a starting point is needed at the ground level is good enough.

When you first think of Macintosh, you will more than likely have the word *COMPUTER* pop into your mind. Well, it should. But do you really understand the word? There are many definitions for the word, ranging from someone who can add columns quickly (that's where the word came from), to a definition that brings in bits, bytes and all that other technical gobble-degook. For the purposes of this book, and for the Macintosh, *COMPUTER* means an information tool—an extension of the mind, a device that allows you to extend your sixth sense—your ability to think, reason and make decisions. When you define computer this way, it is more friendly.

We are going to assume that you have taken your Mac home and removed it from its box. You're probably struck by the fact that it's a soft creamy brown and isn't very intimidating. Before you is a grayish-like surface that, in "techy" terms, is called a **CRT** or **CATHODE RAY TUBE**. Sometimes you hear this called a screen, and that the screen is made up of picture elements or pixels, and you probably don't care. That's another reason Mac exists, because the people at Apple realized that you didn't care.

Well, you know that the screen is important, but in that screen there two things: *MENUS* and *WINDOWS. MENUS* allow you to select what you want Mac to do. *WINDOWS* are areas on the screen in which Mac presents information to you.

But Mac's windows are truly magical. For these windows are each linked to one another, and have the ability to overlap.

As with the windows in your house or office, these windows open, close, partly open, and yes, they can break. But unlike a normal window, Mac's windows can change in shape and size. They can hold large pieces of information or they can be filled with relatively tiny morsels.

As you are exploring your Mac, you have before you two other devices: the *KEYBOARD* and *MOUSE*. Of course you know all about the keyboard—we did spend a great deal of time explaining it to you earlier. It is reasonably familiar since it looks a great deal like the keyboard of your typewriter. But Mac's keyboard is more than an electronic typewriter. Think of it as an extension of your fingers—deep into the mind of the machine.

Working with the keyboard is the mouse. In a way, it is much like the furry little critter that you might have as a pet. But MacMouse is a special tool that allows you to manipulate the information available in the Mac Window. It is, for all practical purposes, another form of a pen or pencil, paint brush, spray can, or piece of chalk. You can do everything with MacMouse that you can do with any of these other "tools".

With the mouse and keyboard firmly embedded in your mind, there is the word *PARADIGM*. For fun, you might want to run to your dictionary and look up the definition. You'll quickly find that it appears to have no meaning that could be related to computers that is readily discernible. Yet in fact, it is almost a perfect word when used in concert with Macintosh since it basically means the perturbation—alteration—of any given set of actions.

Therefore, a MacParadigm denotes a selection of an action or information and its manipulation in some manner. You select and react—you follow a direct line of actions related to one thing. If you're an Apple fan, you would know that the idea is one person, one machine, one task.

Macintosh embellishes this a great deal, and although a single task machine, it does allow you to select from a universe of functions, such as writing, painting, communications, and even programming—all appearing available at the same time.

Now that we've got you moving along at a steady clip, let's keep the momentum going.

When you convey information to another knowledge worker, you usually carry on some form of dialogue. You're familiar with that word and the concept. Since you are, Apple decided that it was a good idea to use it to create a method whereby you could carry on an almost human conversation with Macintosh. The method chosen was the *DIALOG BOX* that we've discussed in several chapters. Now you know what they really are: conversation pieces.

There is another word and concept left to be discussed: *ICON*. Now an *ICON* is a special beast. It is a graphic representation of an action or function to be taken. The Europeans like icons since they solve the language problem. A symbol of a circled truck with a line through it means trucks aren't allowed. With Mac, a symbol of a phone set denotes a modem, and a symbol for a trash can denotes a place to throw old information.

The concept of the *ICON* is closely coupled with paradigm since they go hand-in-hand. Choose, select, manipulate. You choose by pointing to a symbol which you then select by clicking (this is the same as depressing the button) the mouse. Then you use either the keyboard or mouse to perform some action on the information.

Another way you can think about all these terms we've defined so far is as a legend on a road map. And consider the road map very well done. It's easy to read, follow, and has many routes by which you can retrace your steps. Plus it is easy to fold back up and put away.

You read in an earlier chapter that you could change the shape or size of a window, or move objects, or move the position of a window on the screen. This was achieved by using *SCROLL BARS, SIZE BOXES, TITLE AREAS* and other sensitive areas of the screen. Further, by *DRAGGING*, you could move things another location, or stretch them out. You see, certain places on the screen have a meaning to Mac. When you point to one of these areas, Mac interprets this to mean you wish to perform some action.

Notice that all the words, phrases, and concepts are basically the same words you use everyday. That's fun, and that's what makes Mac a useful tool.

Although in the Foreword of this book we said this wasn't a computer book, the fact of the matter is that it really is. We waited until now to say that so you would enjoy the book more as a novel. And since it really is a computer book, common sense (after all, that is really what Mac is all about) dictates that we define at least one really technical term. Therefore, we've decided on **MICROPROCESSOR.**

In this most frivolous of definitions, **MICROPROCESSOR** means something that processes micros. This doesn't make any sense whatsoever. Believe it or not, unless you are really into technical matters, the real definition isn't much more coherent.

You really don't need to know, nor should you care about microprocessors—you may, however, be interested to know that the Mac uses a Motorola 68000 (see Appendix A). This device forms the thinking heart of Mac—or should we say core?

This processor is extremely powerful and is roughly equivalent to the power of a computer that once took up a whole room. Within the Mac, this processor serves a number of functions such as the main computer engine; it also keeps things happening on the screen as well as watching for information that comes in from other sources, such as the mouse and modem. In addition, it talks to the disk drive via another special processor.

All of the actual computer type operations are transparent to you. All that you see are the results—which was the plan in the first place. Maybe this isn't a computer book after all.

There is one final term you should acquaint yourself with: **MASS STORAGE.** Now this doesn't mean a large garage, but it does mean a place to keep a great deal of information. The Macintosh uses a device called a disk drive, but a very special one called a microdrive, and it happens to be made by Sony, the same people who possibly made your television or the radio you have tucked in your belt.

This drive is very tiny and uses a special disk or media housed in a rigid plastic shell. You can stuff as much as 400,000 pieces of information in one of these tiny packages and carry it away in your pocket without fear of destroying the information.

INDEX

APPLE INTERFACING 🐞

Brings you real, tested interfacing circuits that work, plus the necessary BASIC software to connect your Apple to the outside world. Lets you control other devices and communicate with other computers, modems, serial printers, and more! By Jonathan A. Titus, David G. Larsen, and Christopher A. Titus. 208 pages, 5½ x 8½, soft. ISBN 0-672-21862-3. © 1981.
No. 21862 . . . . $11.95

INTIMATE INSTRUCTIONS IN INTEGER BASIC

Explains flowcharting, loops, functions, graphics, variables, and more as they relate to Integer BASIC. Used with *Applesoft Language* (No. 22073), it gives you everything you need to program BASIC with your Apple II or Apple II Plus. By Brian D. Blackwood and George H. Blackwood. 160 pages, 5½ x 8½, soft. ISBN 0-672-21812-7. © 1981.
No. 21812 . . . . $8.95

MOSTLY BASIC: APPLICATIONS FOR YOUR APPLE II, BOOK 1

Twenty-eight debugged, fun-and-serious BASIC programs you can use immediately on your Apple II. Includes a telephone dialer, digital stopwatch, utilities, games, and more. By Howard Berenbon. 160 pages, 8½ x 11, comb. ISBN 0-672-21789-9. © 1980.
No. 21789 . . . . $13.95

MOSTLY BASIC: APPLICATIONS FOR YOUR APPLE II, BOOK 2

A second gold mine of fascinating BASIC programs for your Apple II, featuring 3 dungeons, 11 household programs, 6 on money or investment, 2 to test your ESP level, and more — 32 in all! By Howard Berenbon. 224 pages, 8½ x 11, comb. ISBN 0-672-21864-X. © 1981.
No. 21864 . . . . $12.95

SAMS SOFTWARE FOR THE APPLE

FINANCIAL PLANNING FOR VISICALC® AND THE APPLE II

Automatically sets up your VisiCalc spreadsheet to perform 16 different calculations commonly needed in business and financial planning, and lets you compare as many as four possibilities. Works with 80-column board if you have one. You'll neeed VisiCalc, 64K RAM one disk drive, and DOS 3.3. ISBN 0-672-29059-6.
No. 29059 . . . . $79.95

FINANCIAL PLANNING FOR MULTIPLAN™ AND THE APPLE II

Same as *Financial Planning for VisiCalc* except works with Multiplan spreadsheet, 64K RAM, one disk drive and DOS 3.3. ISBN 0-672-29058-8.
No. 29058 . . . . $79.95

MONEY TOOL

Helps you manage income, expenses, and tax information for home or small business. Can reconcile checking, provide simple reports, and more. By Herb Honig. Requires 48K RAM, Applesoft in ROM and one disk drive and DOS 3.3. ISBN 0-672-26113-8.
No. 26113 . . . . $59.95

FINANCIAL FACTS

Instantly computes the majority of data you'll commonly need in personal and small-business financial management, and prints out the major factors. By Ed Hanson. Requires 48K RAM, Applesoft in ROM, and one disk drive. ISBN 0-672-26099-9.
No. 26099 . . . . $59.95

INSTANT RECALL™

Friendly, unconventional, and instantaneous data handler. Each free-form, alphanumeric screenful you enter is an 840-character page you can edit, file, or print out as it appears. By Charles R. Landers. Requires 48K RAM, Applesoft in ROM, one disk drive, and DOS 3.3. ISBN 0-672-26097-2.
No. 26097 . . . . $59.95

PEN-PAL

Sophisticated, powerful, affordable word processor. Provides block movement, line deletion, character and text insertion, and more. Requires 48K RAM, Applesoft in ROM, one disk drive, DOS 3.3 and a printer. ISBN 0-672-26115-4.
No. 26115 . . . . $59.95

HELLO CENTRAL!

Versatile, menu-controlled terminal program you can use with any compatible modem to communicate with networks and other computers. Has built-in text editor, auto dialing, much more. By Bruce Kallick. Requires 48K RAM, Applesoft in ROM, one disk drive, DOS 3.3 and modem. ISBN 0-672-26081-6.
No. 26081 . . . . $99.95